# Step Back

# Step Back

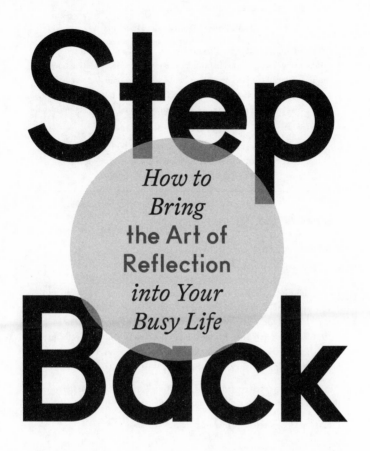

*How to Bring the Art of Reflection into Your Busy Life*

## JOSEPH L. BADARACCO

HARVARD BUSINESS REVIEW PRESS
BOSTON, MASSACHUSETTS

Library of Congress Cataloging-in-Publication Data

Names: Badaracco, Joseph, author.
Title: Step back : how to bring the art of reflection into your busy life / Joseph L. Badaracco.
Description: Boston, MA : Harvard Business Review Press, [2020] | Includes index.
Identifiers: LCCN 2020004737 | ISBN 9781633698741 (hardcover) | ISBN 9781633698758 (ebook)
Subjects: LCSH: Critical thinking. | Well-being. | Success in business.
Classification: LCC BF441 .B254 2020 | DDC 153.4/2—dc23
LC record available at https://lccn.loc.gov/2020004737

ISBN: 978-1-63369-874-1
eISBN: 978-1-63369-875-8

*There are very few human beings who
receive the truth, complete and staggering,
by instant illumination. Most of them
acquire it fragment by fragment, on a
small scale, by successive developments,
cellularly, like a laborious mosaic.*

—The Diary of Anaïs Nin, 1939–1944

# CONTENTS

# Step Back

# 1

# Mosaic Reflection

The founder and CEO of a very successful venture capital firm gives a particular piece of advice to entrepreneurs when his firm invests in their companies. He tells them, "If I ever come into your office and find you looking out the window with your feet up on the desk, I'm going to double your salary."

The CEO was sending two messages, and we all need to hear them. First, reflection is extremely important. In fact, it may be more important now than ever. As our world becomes more complex, fluid, time-pressured, and data-saturated, we need to think deeply about situations, problems, and decisions—at work and throughout the rest of life. The second lesson is that the world today makes it very hard to find time for reflection and might even be eroding our capacity to reflect.

What is reflection? The standard answer appears in familiar images. One is Rodin's famous sculpture, "The Thinker." Another is a Buddhist monk, sitting motionless in meditation. Another may be a solitary figure looking into a starry night sky or a woman with her head bowed in quiet prayer. Thousands of pages have been written about this solitary, deliberate, tranquil approach to reflection. But what is its relevance for people who work and live in a vortex of tasks, meetings, decisions, and serious responsibilities?

Four years ago, I set out to answer that question. I interviewed more than one hundred managers. They ranged from supervisors to CEOs and came from fifteen countries. Most worked in businesses, but the group also included a police chief, heads of several religious organizations, the coach of a major professional sports team, and university administrators. I also carefully studied classic works, like the *Meditations* of Marcus Aurelius and the *Spiritual Exercises* of Ignatius of Loyola, as well as a wide range of diaries and journals.

In the end, I concluded that busy, responsible men and women do make time to reflect—but not during extended periods of solitude. They rely instead on what I came to call "mosaic" reflection. A *mosaic*, of course, is artwork made from small pieces of stone or glass. It also describes what I learned in the interviews: busy, successful men and women do reflect, but they practice the art of reflection in the cracks and crevices of their everyday lives.

Why do they squeeze time for reflection into their already crowded lives? In one interview, a senior manager sketched the basic answer. For several weeks, he had been struggling with the question of whether to change career paths. At one point, he put his decision in a larger context:

> Life is surfing a wave. It carries you forward. You spend most of your time adjusting and trying to stay on the wave and riding it. It may not be the right wave or the right wave anymore, and it may be headed for the rocks. Reflection is thinking about these questions.

This statement points to the basic two reasons why the managers I interviewed tried hard to find time for reflection.

One reason is practical. Reflection is a valuable tool for making better decisions, at work and in the rest of life. It is useful day by day, task by task, and problem by problem. As the senior executive put it, reflection can help you with "adjusting and trying to stay on the wave." As another manager put it, "I always have lingering doubts that I'm not reflecting enough as I handle meeting after meeting."

The other basic reason to reflect is profound. Reflection is a way of grappling with the enduring human questions of how to live, what to really care about, and what counts as a good life. In other words, are you riding "the right wave?" This kind of reflection can make all the difference. In one interview, a former CEO said wistfully, "I wish someone had asked me twenty-five, thirty years ago, 'Are you being true to yourself? Are you giving yourself enough time to reflect?'"

Reflection is stepping back to grasp what really matters—about what you are experiencing, trying to understand, or doing. This is why reflection is remarkably valuable, in so many practical and profound ways. It is crucial to understand what really matters—whether you are running an entire company, leading a task force, navigating the health-care system for an elderly relative, juggling the daily tasks of most households, or struggling with any hard issue.

Throughout this book, you will read, in their own words, how men and women tried, sometimes failed, and often succeeded in finding ways to reflect—on everyday problems, on their careers and families, and on the great, enduring questions of life. As you listen to these men and women, you can respond personally. You can ask yourself questions like these: Is this an obstacle to reflection I often face? Is this an approach to reflection I should try? Am I already doing something along these lines that I could do better?

By answering these questions for yourself, you can develop practical, everyday ways of reflecting that help you work better and live better. This is the aim Marcus Aurelius pursued in writing *Meditations*: "to live in complete consciousness and lucidity; to give each of our instants full intensity; and to give meaning to our entire life."[1]


## Design Principles for Reflection


The art of reflection is like other arts. To do it well, you have to practice, and your practice should be guided by certain principles, which are often called *design princi-ples*. If you paint a picture, for example, you have to make choices about line, balance, and contrast. Design princi-ples call attention to these choices and guide them, but they don't tell you what to paint or what colors to use.[2] Design principles are "laws with leeway."[3] They provide compass directions, not turn-by-turn instructions.

The design principles for reflection work in the same way. If you want to make the best use of scarce time for reflection, you should rely on four basic principles. They clearly define good reflection, but they don't specify what you should do. That is your call. The design principles for the art of reflection are templates, and your task is filling in the specifics, with ways of reflecting that work for you.

The first design principle says: *Aim for good enough*. At first, this principle may sound surprising, even dis-maying. We often hear that if something is worth doing at all, it's worth doing well. In contrast, this principle seems to recommend lowering your standards and slack-ing off. But many things are worth doing or just trying to do, even if you fall short of some ideal, and reflection is one of them—particularly given the many obstacles to reflection we face today.

This design principle advises you to put aside the image of reflection as "going up to the mountain"—that is, as extended, solitary deliberation. Instead, it encourages you to find an approach to reflection that works pretty well, most of the time. This is an approach that meets your needs, fits your situation, and you can follow fairly regularly. But you will have stretches with little or no reflection. That is simply a reality of life, not a failure on your part. When it happens, just move on and get back to your routine of reflection.

But what do you do when you step back and reflect? How do you spend the time well? The answer to this question takes us to the next three design principles. Each describes one of the three fundamental approaches to reflection. These approaches have truly stood the test of time, as measured by centuries and millennia. They also show us the essence of mosaic reflection: spending short periods of time, over the course of days or weeks, relying on your own, personalized combination of these three ways of reflecting.

The first of these design principles says: *Downshift occasionally*. We spend much of our time, particularly at work, relying on highly focused analytical or pragmatic thinking. Our goal is output. We ask, again and again, "What is the problem here, and what do we do about it?" This guiding principle says to pause occasionally and shift your mental machinery into a lower gear. This means, as one manager put it, "letting your mind run free for a while and avoiding any taint of productivity."

Downshifting, in its various forms, gives you greater clarity about what is happening around you and what you are really thinking and feeling. Its aim is depth of experience, and this matters across the board—whether you are running a meeting, talking with a friend, or trying to understand something gnawing at you.

The next principle says: *Ponder your hard issues.* This type of reflection is a way of working through really challenging issues, at work and throughout life. It says to step back and make a conscious effort to look at a problem or a situation from several different perspectives. Pondering can help you gain a fuller understanding of a complex issue and show you which aspects of it really matter.

Pondering is turning something over in your mind, like a woodcarver gradually shaping a piece of wood. One manager gave a succinct, practical definition of pondering. She said, "You've got the linear perspective, which is important, but then you have to develop for yourself a way of finding other angles on things." The aim of pondering is depth of understanding, and the classics and the interviews provide a wide range of ways to do this.

The last design principle says: *Pause and measure up.* This is reflection for times when you have to decide and act. Its focus is depth of impact. It is asking what really matters about what you are doing or planning to do. Pausing to measure up means stepping back for a few moments, looking at your options, and asking yourself what will best meet the standards others expect of you and your own standards for work and life. One manager phrased the question as, "Am I making the difference I'm supposed to make and the difference I really want to make?"

Taken together, the four design principles show us the essence of reflection, whether you reflect for just a few moments or for longer periods. Reflection is stepping back and trying to grasp what really matters about what we are experiencing, thinking, or doing. But when and how should we do this—and how much time do we need to do it well?

Mosaic reflection says you can accomplish a good deal, in moments or minutes, if you understand the fundamental approaches to reflection and if you develop a flexible, working habit of reflective pauses that meshes with your life. Short periods of downshifting, pondering, and measuring up can be combined in many different ways. They are plug-and-play components you can use to create a personal pattern or practice of reflection.

This approach to reflection fits the busy lives so many people lead today. It works especially well for people who find it difficult, because of how their minds work, to withdraw and reflect for extended periods. And the mosaic approach lets us reflect on the flow of life and work and respond to what is real and immediate. One manager put it succinctly, saying, "Sometimes I need to reflect *now*."

Despite its advantages, however, mosaic reflection has a vulnerability: the risk that brief, opportunistic periods of reflection over the course of a day or several days won't provide enough time and continuity for really grappling with serious issues. It may leave you with dispersed and momentary insights—a scattering of mosaic tiles without a purpose or overall pattern.

This is why, from time to time, you need to step back further. This means finding longer periods of time, every few days or certainly every few weeks, for downshifting, pondering, or measuring up, and asking what really matters if you take a broader, longer-term, more deeply personal perspective. In short, the familiar image of extended reflection is hardly outdated. It complements and enhances mosaic reflection.

Each of us is riding our own wave. How do we stay on it? Is it the right wave? How can we use moments of reflection to enhance our work and our lives? To answer these questions, we need to find ways to reflect that mesh with our everyday realities. But how do we do this in a world that seems to be spinning faster and faster?

# Aim for Good Enough

I vividly recall a distressing moment in one of the interviews. A successful senior manager—we will call him Oliver—had just said, emphatically, that reflection was very important to him, professionally and personally. He also said he urged the people working for him to reflect when they faced challenges. But when I asked Oliver how much time he spent on reflection, he said about five minutes a day—on a good day. There were also long stretches, he said, when he was running businesses with urgent problems and he barely reflected at all. Then Oliver leaned forward, stared at me, and said he was going through one of those periods right now. "At the moment," he said, "I am in massive, massive stress."

Oliver had been working hard for several months on a major project, and it seemed to be going nowhere. He was also falling behind on other parts of his job and even on routine emails. Oliver had a résumé of unambiguous accomplishments as CEO of several medium-sized companies in South America. He believed in reflection. What Oliver needed was an approach to reflection that would actually work for him, given the challenges he faced and the life he was actually living. In this respect, he resembled the vast majority of men and women I interviewed. What they needed was a "good enough" approach to reflection.

At first, "good enough" can sound like the wrong way to think about anything important. We wouldn't want to have a "good enough" surgeon operate on us or marry a "good enough" partner. However, given work and life today, "good enough" reflection is a genuine accomplishment.[1] An old Italian adage says, "The better is the enemy of the good," and the first design principle echoes its wisdom.[2]

It says to do what you can. Try to make sure you're spending some time every day or every week doing some form of reflection. From time to time, look for opportunities to do better. But recognize that there will be times when you don't reflect much. That isn't a failure on your part, but simply a reality of life. Your aim is finding and following an approach that works pretty well, at least most of the time.

One manager, who had a very successful track record in both the private and public sectors, described her approach to reflection in this way:

> I may have a good day, a bad day. There may be pressing problems. So, for me, it's being aware that if I haven't had a place to reflect, I probably need to, and I try to create at least a few minutes for that. But I'm not like people who are more disciplined thinkers and can create a calendar that says, "Every day, this is my hour of reflection or meditation or something like that." That's not how my mind works.

This is a description of a flexible, adaptable, "good enough" style of reflection. It describes self-management with a soft touch.

How do you develop your own "good enough" approach? This chapter describes the first step, which is observing yourself and answering two questions: What obstacles to reflection do you regularly confront? And when and how do you manage to overcome them, if only briefly? Once you know this, the next step is using this time well. The next three chapters will show you specific ways to do this, by relying on the three other design principles for reflection.

## What Are Your Obstacles to Reflection?

A memorable line from the classic movie *Casablanca* is, "Round up the usual suspects."[3] In the case of reflection, there is now a standard list of reasons why we don't reflect more often: an intensely competitive economy, flatter and leaner organizations, insecure jobs, and technology that erases the boundary between work and leisure. In essence, we are all hired hands working on fast-moving, digital conveyor belts—with little time for family, friends, and sleep, much less reflection. Even worse, when we do have leisure, we are mesmerized by seductive, ingeniously designed interfaces and compulsively click away our "free" time.

This explanation is all too true, and our everyday experience confirms it. But this conventional wisdom is also incomplete and misleading. It is hard to find time for reflection, but the reason isn't simply workplace pressure and irresistible, omnipresent technology. The obstacles run deeper, and this is a reality almost everyone has to face.

To see why, turn the clock back for a moment. In the mid-1800s, the New England poet and essayist Henry David Thoreau feared that a new technology—small-scale, slow-moving, primitive railroads—was dramatically accelerating and distorting how people worked and lived. "We do not ride on the railroad," Thoreau wrote, "it rides upon us."[4] His European contemporary, the German philosopher and essayist Arthur Schopenhauer, had similar fears. "To live at random in the hurly-burly of business or pleasure," he wrote, "without ever reflecting upon the past—to go on, as it were, pulling cotton off the reel of life—is to have no clear idea of what we are about."[5]

Thoreau and Schopenhauer, like many others in the long history of serious thought about reflection, confronted obstacles to reflection that predate global capitalism, the internet, and smartphones. A recent history has traced concerns about exhaustion, its causes, and its implications over two millennia, indicating that contemporary technologies and workplaces aren't the full explanation of why we don't reflect more often.[6] They seem to act as accelerants, intensifying fires they did not ignite.

Like Oliver, the managers interviewed for this study weren't galley slaves on Roman triremes. They had chosen their jobs and had significant control over their daily schedules. There were other, deeper factors that kept them—and keep us—from spending more time reflecting. As you read about these deeper factors, you can think about which ones are particularly challenging for you.

## Serious Commitments

Oliver understood quite clearly that there was a deeper reason why he didn't reflect, and he stated it succinctly:

> Work, work, work. That's who I am. And all the time, I'm enjoying it and it's purposeful and it's good. I think all human beings have an insatiable desire to build, assuming they've met their primal needs. There is real satisfaction from doing things and having a queue of things to do that you think are important.

The managers I interviewed had made thoughtful choices about how they wanted to live their lives and what they wanted to accomplish. Day by day, these managers typically felt acute time pressure. Their work seemed to be a struggle. It tired them out and wore them down. They wondered at times if this was how they want to spend their lives. But that was only one side of a coin. The other side consisted of their responsibilities and commitments to others. At a deeper level, they were also making good on commitments to themselves. They often had demanding standards that they really wanted to meet, standards for how they wanted to work and live.

In most cases, these men and women had other serious responsibilities at home and sometimes in their communities. As a result, their personal time management efforts became triage programs, and they left possible periods of reflection on the battlefield. One manager said simply, "I go from commitments at home to commitments at work to commitments to volunteer organizations, so I have very little me time." Another, who thought of reflection as prayer, said regretfully, "I just don't make time to nurture that relationship with God. I wait until the end of the day, and then I'm tired, and will be like five sentences to God, which is not the basis of a robust prayer life, and I know I need to get better at that."

Those comments came from middle managers. In most cases, entrepreneurs have chosen to take on even more demanding responsibilities. They understand that their embryonic businesses are fragile, that a decision by one big customer can be crucial to its survival, and that most new businesses fail. Yet they are intensely committed to this work. It is central to their identities. As one entrepreneur put it, looking back on the challenges of his early years, "The joy of life is in the struggle."

The CEOs I interviewed also felt they didn't have enough time to reflect because of pressures they faced and serious commitments they had made, which involved the livelihoods of hundreds or thousands of people. One CEO said, "I just felt that no matter what I was doing, I was always getting pulled somewhere else. It seems like I was always cheating someone—my company, my family, myself. I couldn't truly focus on anything."[7]

And senior executives have it easy compared with the women and men who are single parents trying to support their families with minimum-wage jobs. A senior executive on a chauffeured trip to the airport can put down his or her cell phone, gaze through a tinted window, and reflect on challenges at work or at home. This option isn't available to people riding in crowded public transportation and preoccupied with having enough cash to pay the week's bills. In fact, recent studies indicate that poverty erodes the capacity for certain kinds of serious thinking.[8]

These are all versions of Oliver's predicament: he believed reflection was worthwhile but he could rarely find more than five minutes a day to do it, largely because he was a hard worker, regularly said yes to demanding assignments and new challenges, and cared deeply about doing them well. These traits are truly praiseworthy, but they squeezed down time for reflection.

A standard piece of advice for men and women who are overcommitted is to tell them to prioritize and reduce their commitments. In many cases, this is worth thinking about, but the problem runs deeper—and, for some people, an intensely committed life isn't a problem. It's how they want to live. One manager put it simply, saying, "I tend to run toward crises—that's what gets me jazzed."

## The Productivity Cult

The logical reaction to the combination of workplace pressures and serious personal commitments is to look for ways to be more productive. This means figuring out what really needs doing and then doing it as efficiently as possible. Unfortunately, however, this sensible response carries the risk of gradually turning a person into a full-fledged member of the cult of productivity. Its adherents feel that, if they aren't being productive, the world is out of whack and they shouldn't feel good about themselves.

This was an explicit theme in several of the interviews. One manager said, "I hate feeling idle. I hate the feeling of not doing anything that I don't think is productive. I have a feeling that reflection on my own is not productive." Another said, "I feel like today is wasting away if I'm not doing something."

It has long been said that the job shapes the person, and this phenomenon is easy to joke about. An example is the consultant whose teenager asks him about a personal problem and who replies by diagramming the boy's concerns on a $2 \times 2$ matrix. Another example is the hedge fund manager who, to the dismay of his wife, told their children that certain activities weren't "bonus behavior."

These are amusing stories, but the French have a phrase that points to its underlying risk. The phrase is *deformation professionelle*. This is skewing how you think and live based on whatever leads to success at work. A senior manager had this description of how he felt after stepping down from a demanding position. "I had a kind of PTSD," he said, "because my inbox and text messages gave me a clear sense that I was needed, and I felt addicted to being needed." Oliver's version of this was, "I love to put out fires, and I love getting things done."

The cult of productivity eviscerates true leisure, which exempts you from accountability about how you spend time. In other words, you don't have to have anything to "show for it." An old Italian saying, "Dolce far niente" or "It is sweet to do nothing," exactly expresses this philosophy of leisure. But this notion evaporates when occupational habits become all-encompassing and nearly everything we do is governed by the standard of output. As one manager put it regretfully, "Sometimes I'm afraid that productivity and control, or the illusion of control, are the default conditions of my life." And this problem may be worse for younger generations. A recent study concluded that many young people view hyper-busyness as an "aspirational lifestyle."[9]

What about just going home and closing the door on the day's work? The problem is that the mental habits of successful work are indeed habits. We follow them almost automatically and feel bad if we don't. The archetypal "organization man" of the 1950s dealt with this problem by starting his evening with a couple of martinis, but he didn't have the option of pulling out a device and continuing the day's work. As one manager put it:

> I think that some people imagine that if you have enough mental discipline, you can flip the switch in your head and, wherever you are, you can go from work to reflection, and I don't think that's true. I don't think there is a switch. Also, I usually get home and don't feel it's OK to take the time to slow down because I feel I really should be busy doing things. Also, people from work are still waiting and expecting things.

## Deeper Discomfort

The painter Edgar Degas observed, "There is a kind of success that is indistinguishable from panic."[10] The idea is that ceaseless work can serve as a powerful distraction and anesthetic—a self-administered drug we take when we sense that pausing for reflection would be uncomfortable. One manager put it this way:

> I don't like reflecting on the past. I didn't have a happy childhood, so I think looking back is not

something I'm comfortable doing. And so I have always been a forward-looking person and very goal-oriented. What's the next hurdle I'm going to get over, and what's the next step I'm going to take or the next thing I'm going to achieve? Task, task, task.

The interviews indicated that this obstacle to reflection takes many different forms. Sometimes it's a way of avoiding challenging everyday issues. One manager said he observed the problem frequently and directly:

I think reflection is hard, and I think it makes people who are goal-oriented anxious. I will often see in meetings that people, when subjects get hard, kind of reflexively reach for their iPhones and start checking their calendars and doing something else because it's relieving to them. They want to stay out of the stickiness.

Sometimes the anxiety comes from looking down the road and grappling with what lies in the future. A former CEO acknowledged in personal terms the discomfort reflection can cause because it can involve thinking about long-term, high-stakes, uncertain choices. In another interview, you can see how a very accomplished and poised individual moved from "unsettling" to "frightening" as he talked about reflection at work:

> It is sometimes unsettling to make that space
> and make that time and build it in or get your
> secretary not to fill every minute in—it can be a
> little frightening because, you know, this is the
> time when I'm supposed to sit down with a pad
> of paper and really think ahead and you'd much
> rather be busy because it's so easy to focus on
> the latest emails. Some of the crazy busyness is
> self-imposed.

Other managers said reflection threatened to expose feelings of vulnerability. A middle-aged manager put it this way, "I consider reflection is just kind of getting through the emotional stuff and maybe not being so afraid, I guess, to fail." Sometimes the reluctance to reflect involves simply getting through the day. As one very successful consultant put it, "There's the fragility of the self-image. Most people shy away from the reality— and all of us, myself included, are more content to hold on to a fictionalized view of ourselves that we hold dear rather than confront any of the reality that may differ from that fictionalized account." One manager was apprehensive about looking at some aspects of the recent past, saying, "The pain and fear of reflection result from the pain and fear of having been wrong."

## Our Hypervigilant Brains

The deepest obstacle to reflection may be a permanent feature of our minds. They are restless. Our thoughts zigzag almost constantly. Extended moments of clarity and control are the exceptions and hardly the rule. As a result, it is very difficult, even if you have plenty of time, to reflect in the calm, focused, extended way that the familiar image shows us.

A poignant example of this occurred in an interview with a CEO. This was one of the times in my interviews when the person I was speaking with was basically reflecting aloud. Here is a little literal transcript of what he said, "I've been working hard on an important presentation about the lessons I've learned and we've learned at the company over the last five years. And, between us, my father passed yesterday after a series of strokes last weekend. I think I've now retraced every fish we caught and every goose we shot since I was a kid." Notice how abruptly his thinking and perhaps his feelings jumped from the presentation to his father. This unexpected and unconnected shift in his thinking, which leapt across topics and time, turned out to be an important topic in our interview.

You can see how restless our minds are by trying the simple experiment. Stop reading and spend a minute or two observing what goes through your mind. Or take another minute and try to concentrate on something specific, like your breath or an object in the room. You will soon experience a deep-seated obstacle to reflection. The early Buddhists described it by saying we have "monkey minds" that shift constantly from thought to thought.

Why is it so difficult to control our attention and focus our minds? The fundamental answer may be evolutionary design. The prehuman creatures who were acutely alert were more likely to survive. They were the first to notice the saber-toothed tiger stealthily approaching their encampment; the tiny, deadly insect crawling on their offspring; or a subtle sign of toxicity in a plant or carcass they were about to eat. In the end, the prehumans who were vigilant, acute, continuous scanners outsurvived their sluggish-minded contemporaries, and over eons they evolved into us. In short, the Buddhist depiction of monkey minds describes not only our quicksilver attention, but also its evolutionary origin.

The obstacles to reflection clearly run deep. Nevertheless, virtually all of the managers found at least some time for reflection, despite their frenetic lives. Sometimes they put their phones down for a moment of peace, but there was no off-switch for their serious commitments, their instinct to be useful and productive, their all-too-human reluctance to dwell on hard personal issues, or the hypervigilant operating systems evolution had installed in their brains.

So when and how did the managers succeed in stepping back? They didn't rely on iron discipline, rigid scheduling, or frequent retreats into solitude. In fact, they didn't attack the obstacles directly. Instead of trying to blast tunnels through the mountain ranges of obstacles, they looked for gaps and passageways. This is an approach that you can follow to create your own "good enough" mosaic of reflective moments.

## When Do You Overcome Your Obstacles to Reflection?

Many of the interviews started in a similar way. The individuals I was meeting would say they were probably the wrong person for the interview because they didn't

spend much time reflecting. As the conversation contin-
ued, however, almost everyone mentioned a few times
when they did reflect, over the course of most days or
weeks. In addition, I had a second interview with more
than half of the managers, usually about ten days after
the first interview, and they typically reported other
times and places when they had paused for reflection.
Several ultimately said something like, "I guess I spend
more time reflecting than I realized."

What was going on here? First, when managers ini-
tially said they didn't reflect very much, they meant they
didn't reflect for extended periods on a regular basis. In
other words, they weren't following the standard model
of reflection. Second, when they did reflect, the managers relied on a wide variety of approaches, but they
assumed that these were just their own ad hoc, idiosyn-
cratic ways of reflecting.

In reality, however, they were reflecting in useful and
sometimes valuable ways. There were times over the
course of a day or a week when they managed to work
their way around the obstacles to reflection they faced.
They had developed practical ways to escape the magnetic pull of their smartphones and slow the gyrations of
their minds. They put down the challenges and burdens
of their serious commitments. They stopped optimizing

productivity. And at times they even managed to touch on uncomfortable topics.

It was as if they—and we—have a strong, innate impulse to reflect. Perhaps the prehumans who paused from time to time and assessed what was happening around them were more likely to survive and hence evolved into us. Whatever the explanation, the interviews suggest that moments of reflection somehow work their way into the gaps and fissures of busy lives.

To find these moments of reflection, you have to observe yourself. The interviews suggest looking in five directions and, as you do this, asking yourself two questions: "Would something along these lines work for me?" and "Do I already do some version of this that I can extend and build on?"

WHEN AND WHERE. If you think about the last few days or the last week, what were you doing at the times when you felt you were stepping back, if only briefly, and reflecting? This question asks you to notice what you were doing, physically, and where you were, physically, when you managed to push past your obstacles to reflection and step back for a moment.

We reflect with our minds, so it is easy to ignore the plain fact that our minds are embedded in our brains and our brains are hardwired to our nervous systems and senses. Our bodies are the ecosystem of our minds. Hence, changes in physical space and different physical postures affect our minds, often in significant but unnoticed ways.

This probably explains why, when the managers reflected, most of them stepped back literally. That is, they put some physical distance between themselves and their routine daily activities. One manager said, "I've always found that the environmentals are important. Even if I have the time, I can't just plop myself anywhere and reflect, so I think I contemplate what's the right environment." Another said, "I need to create sacred places and sacred spaces for myself."

Even the minimalist advice of the venture capitalist—"If I catch you with your feet on your desk and I see you looking out the window"—involves a shift of physical position and focus. Several of the managers said they did something along the same lines, without even leaving their offices. One woman said, "I'll sit on the sofa sometimes, so I'm not sucked into doing whatever is on my desk, or I'll stand by the window sometimes, just to change the scenery a little bit, and get out the reactive mode."

It is no accident that so many of the great religious traditions ask their followers to go to a special place of worship and then, in many cases, follow some sequence of standing, sitting, kneeling, singing and chanting, or conscious breathing as part of their reflective practices. The same approach appears outside of traditional religious practice, as in many contemporary meditative practices.

There is an important, underlying reason to step back in some physical way—to turn off the computer monitor, look out the window, close your eyes, take a short walk, or simply try to breathe more slowly. Sitting at a desk and working on a computer or sitting in a meeting call for a particular kind of focused attention and systematic thought. Over time, particular mental activities can become closely and habitually associated with particular physical activities. It becomes easier to think in certain ways when we are in certain places or doing certain things.

Virtually all of the managers interviewed for this study had discovered times and places that allowed them to step back from the merry-go-rounds of their daily lives, if only briefly and incompletely, and spend a little time reflecting. Over months or years, they gradually learned what worked for them—not automatically, but fairly often and fairly well. And what mattered in general was what came naturally to them or even what they enjoyed, which made it easier for them to overcome the daunting obstacles to reflection.

PIGGYBACKED REFLECTION. Roughly fifteen of the managers reflected in a surprising way: while they were engaged—or, more precisely, partially engaged—in another, unrelated activity. This meant "stepping back" from these activities by paying only low-level attention to them and focusing their primary attention on some larger question or issue. The two most common were exercising and commuting to work by car, but this approach to reflection also took many other forms.

At first, this way of reflecting looks like a mistake. It seems to be a version of multitasking, which often means doing two things simultaneously and poorly. But, for the most part, the managers typically insisted that this approach was valuable and, when pressed, they typically said they weren't really doing two different things at once. Their explanation, to use a computer analogy, was that the routine, repetitive task was "running in the background," while they focused on some significant or serious issue that had been triaged out of their busy days.

Several also insisted that piggybacking reflection on top of certain other activities actually enhanced reflection. Two advocates of reflection believed that vigorous exercise did this by improving blood flow to their brains. Others felt that the right level of distraction somehow enabled valuable thoughts and feelings to come forward from the back of their minds. One of the managers said, "You get tired after a while, and then your rational, emotional filters go away a little bit and you can see some things or deal with some things that you usually avoid."

One manager was quite explicit about how he used his time running. He said that he often was in situations where he had read everything relevant and spoken to everyone he should have consulted and now needed to make a decision. His runs were ways of doing this. He didn't have a schedule or to-do list in front of him, he was already being "productive" by getting out and exercising, and the low-level distraction of running might have freed his mind to see an issue from new perspectives. George Sheehan, a physician and well-known writer on running, suggested that the right exercise could help individuals reflect in important ways when he wrote, "The first 30 minutes of running is for my body and the second 30 minutes is for my soul."[11]

The other common type of piggybacked reflection was commuting to and from work. This was surprising, because most of the managers commuted by car and were presumably focused on driving carefully. The

typical pattern involved commutes of thirty to sixty minutes each way, often in slow traffic. The individuals who
did this usually said they began their trips by listening to
music, news, or talk on the radio and then, after a while,
turning the radio off and reflecting on pressing work
issues. But these, in turn, often opened up into broader
issues, professional and personal.

For example, one manager said:

My car ride home is slow, and I guess it's when I
do unstructured reflection. I drive with pads of
paper, and I'll write down everything when I'm
thinking about something. When I drive, I never
listen to music or talk. I think that in the car, I
find it really easy to concentrate because there's
nobody talking to me, and you can watch the
road, which I think you can do with about half
your brain, while the other half is at work.

When the managers were asked skeptical questions
about how well they could reflect while driving or how
safely they could drive while thinking about something
else, they responded that this simply wasn't a problem for
them, particularly in slow traffic, and that commuting
time was a good opportunity for reflection. One man-

ager said, "Having some level of background effort expenditure allows your mind to really think about things."

These managers also described personal variations on reflecting while driving. These are good examples of the many ways in which you can customize and personalize mosaic reflection. For example, several of the managers assigned themselves specific questions to think about during their commute, while others focused on whatever occurred to them. Some made simple notes on paper, while others dictated into their smartphones. And one unusual approach to reflection while driving came from a younger manager, who said she reflected while traveling to and from work, and then referred to her father, who was a farmer, by saying, "My father says he doesn't go to church, because he does a lot of thinking on the tractor."

In addition to reflection during exercise and commuting, several managers mentioned that they got good ideas while taking showers, and a Japanese manager put this somewhat poignantly, saying, "What I suffer when I travel is that there's no bathtub. When you are in the bath, warm, you are alone, very quiet, you can again go through lots of things."

The managers who relied on the piggyback approach believed they were primarily focused on reflection. Their approach may be a contemporary, secular version of repetitive religious rituals, like chanting or saying a rosary, that have been practiced in many faiths for millennia. Most important, these blended or piggybacked reflections worked pretty well for many of the managers, enabling them to do more reflection than they otherwise would.

THE RIGHT CONVERSATION. If you put aside the familiar image of solitary reflection, you will find another approach—a reflective conversation with another person—that is well worth learning and using. Roughly a fifth of the managers said they relied on a version of this kind of reflection from time to time. For them, reflection was social rather than solitary.

A reflective conversation requires the right partner, but how do you know who this is? The interviews suggested that the answer is somewhat intangible. In other words, you simply know. "When we sit down," one manager said about a trusted confidant at work, "there's a different atmosphere, and we can really talk." But the interviews also pointed to several characteristics of the right person.

Often, the right person is someone you know pretty well, through shared experiences at work or in life. For one manager, the right person was her father. "It's just talking about the day," she said, "and I talk to him every day. My commute is about forty-five minutes. He's probably the person that I verbally reflect with the most." A young manager, who worked in finance, said he had similar conversations with his mother several times a week. And several managers knew someone at work who, as one put it, was "the kind of person you go see when you need to talk something through, so you go to their office and close the door."

Shared experiences aren't, however, the whole story. The decisive factor is a feeling of personal connection—a sense that someone is, in the words of one manager, "simpatico, but in a deeper way." Conversations with this person move comfortably to more important or serious issues. They move past the events of the day and what one manager called, "deeply shallow talk that seems friendly and personal but doesn't fill you up and you don't feel more connected."

Sometimes the right person has a talent for asking the right questions. As one manager put it, "You need someone you trust to ask you the kinds of questions that you might find too challenging and you might half wish they hadn't asked you, but you realize afterwards that it was what you needed." One manager described a former boss as a master of the art of reflective conversations, saying:

> I'd say he didn't give me any advice at all, and much later, when I got smarter and I was trying to lead people, I thought it's really dangerous to actually ask questions, because what people need is a space to reflect. Your acting is kind of a mirror to help them see what they're doing and what the problems are. It's a matter of responding, usually subtly, and showing them that you care, even through body language, and just asking good clarifying questions. You're trying in the most delicate fashion to help other people fit things together.

Sometimes the questions you need to hear come from someone whose experiences and perspectives differ from yours, but are complementary. One manager said, "I'm lucky, and my husband has been an amazing partner for me, and we have a lot of ongoing dialogue about the progress of the kids and my work problems. And he knows I'm overanalytical about things and he balances that."

As with the other approaches to reflection, it is important to develop your own personal, hybrid approach to these conversations. For example, a former executive at a major US retailer relied on a particular combination of writing and conversation:

> I do all of the upfront stuff by myself. I don't talk to anybody about it at all. Not my spouse, not a friend. I write on yellow pads, and I try to identify variables and things I'm thinking about, things I like and things I don't like, trying to see if some patterns emerge, and I don't engage in translating the reflection into conversation and decision making until I have narrowed the messiness. I do want help, but I believe I owe the people I'm going to talk with not to do a complete data dump. These are not therapists, and so I want to organize the stuff.

Another alternative is a reflective conversation with the right group, rather than the right person. The sense of personal connection, trust, and empathy still matters—as it does in all reflective conversations—but the setting is different. For example, one manager said she met every few weeks with a group of "good professional friends," and they often talked about issues that were bothering or distressing them. Another manager said he and several friends tried to go out for drinks right after work every few weeks. He said they spent a few minutes talking about sports but felt they could put "hard work problems and even some personal issues on the table."

The interviews show that you can have reflective conversations at the office, at home, at restaurants, and in many other settings. You can talk about a wide range of topics. The conversations don't have to be regular and don't have to follow any particular format. They simply have to be "good enough." This means they help you make some progress on a problem or a concern, because a sense of trust, confidence, and understanding permeates the conversation.

WRITING. Another "good enough" way of reflecting—a tactic that roughly a quarter of the managers relied on—was doing some form of occasional writing. How often they did this depended on their inclinations and schedules. None of the managers said they sat down and wrote on a regular or frequent basis. Instead, they spent a little time writing when they felt the need to do it. As one manager put it, "I have a personal journal and maybe every three months, if I'm honest in how often I actually sit down and write in it, I try to say where I am professionally and in my personal relationships."

As with other forms of "good enough" reflection, the interviews made clear that you can rely on a wide range of personalized approaches for written reflections. Most of the managers who kept journals wrote in them by hand—because they felt it slowed them down and made them a little more reflective—and one manager said he kept his religious reflections online. His "searchable reflections," he said, made it easy to go back and find the times in his life when he was thinking about a particular issue.

Another option is what is called a "commonplace book." One manager said, "I keep this journal, and when I run across things I read or hear or get sent to me or whatever that I find inspirational or thought-provoking, then I write them in the book. I've kept it since college and it's brown leather, and I probably have a couple hundred pages and I do go back and read that from time to time."

The interviews clearly indicate that, to find a personalized approach that works for you, it is important to think imaginatively and move beyond the traditional approaches to journals and diaries. One option, as one manager put it, is "carrying notebooks all over the place and do little bits of writing all the time." Another used paper to quickly get down messy, initial thoughts—what he called "a collection of random synaptic impulses on paper." And a young engineer wrote on spreadsheets when she had to make decisions because, "I feel like, at my core, I'm an engineer. So I analyze things. I try to break things down to the root causes."

These unusual approaches to written reflections point toward the many other personalized, "good enough" approaches to reflection that appeared in the interviews. One manager tried to create short "bookends" at the beginning and end of each day to reflect on what she had accomplished and what still needed doing. Some of the religious managers tried to read the Bible for a few minutes on most mornings, and the CEO of a *Fortune* 50 company utilized an online program that provided a daily biblical passage and initial reflections on it. One manager found she could reflect well when she was working on her hobby of creating art installations. Another consciously tried to avoid other people when he walked his dog because this was one of his best times for reflection.

How did these managers develop their flexible, customized, "good enough" approaches to reflection? In some cases, they consciously experimented. A very successful manager had meditated daily for years—because his wife pushed him to attend a weekend seminar on the topic. He went reluctantly and became a convert. In contrast, another individual, a senior McKinsey partner, said, "I have a friend who runs a major personnel firm, and he'll tell me he went on a twenty-four-hour retreat that was so wonderful, and my reaction is 'Not in a hundred years.' I'm just not the kind of person who goes off and does things like that."

Overall, however, conscious experimentation was the exception, not the rule. Most managers simply became aware, over time and through self-observation, that certain routines worked for them. They tried to follow these routines, but they weren't set in stone. As their lives and work changed, the managers adapted their routines. "One of my life goals," said a retired HR manager, "is to figure out what my patterns are and which ones work for me and which ones don't work for me."

## Does "Good Enough" Work?

It is natural to be skeptical about "good enough" reflection. Maybe it is a second-best approach, forced on us by the demands of life and work today. But the reality is that men and women who take their responsibilities seriously have always had long days and nights of serious work. For them, time for reflection has always been a scarce commodity. This is why some of the important figures in the long history of reflection have relied on flexible, sometimes opportunistic approaches to think deeply about their lives and their work.

Consider, for example, a remarkable document written by the Roman emperor Marcus Aurelius. It has been published countless times, in the form of a short book entitled *Meditations*, but the original document was merely his personal notebook. In fact, the more accurate title for it is an earlier one—"To Himself"—because the document is simply a record of Marcus's private reflections and was never intended for publication.

*Meditations* shows us that, despite its vulnerabilities, mosaic reflection can be a valuable way of stepping back, thinking deeply, and finding ways past the obstacles to reflection. Despite his intermittent efforts, Marcus was able to return again and again to themes and questions he really cared about. His occasional, fragmentary reflections produced a work that has truly stood the test of time. For centuries, countless men and women in all walks of life have turned to him for guidance, solace, and wisdom.

Marcus kept this journal while he shouldered enormous responsibilities. He was leading what became a thirteen-year campaign against German tribes trying to invade the Roman empire. For long stretches, Marcus lived in a tent, with only campfire heat, often in dismal, swampy conditions, near the Danube River. It was a life without the leisure, comfort, and wealth to which Roman emperors were accustomed. And, while Marcus was immersed in military life and responsibilities, the plague was ravaging Rome, killing as many as a third of its citizens, and political rivals were conspiring against him. One biographer observed that Marcus lacked "the kiss of the fairy"—a natural gift for ease, laughter, and pleasure. His tenacious devotion to duty may have ruined his health and caused him to die from exhaustion.[12]

Yet this heavily burdened, hardworking individual found time for reflection. Historians don't know when and how he wrote *Meditations*, but it is short—most editions are roughly one hundred pages long—and it consists of brief entries, organized very loosely into twelve chapters. The entries follow the rapidly shifting flow of Marcus's thoughts. In a paragraph or two, he will move among observations about other people, reflections on nature, admonitions to himself about his failings and how he wants to live, lessons from his teachers, and other topics. His reflections seem to have been written in brief snatches of time, perhaps in the evenings, when

Marcus could take a break from his duties and when he had the energy to write.

Marcus did what many of the managers in the study tried to do. He seized moments of opportunity for reflection in his busy life. He even had a name for these moments: they were his "spaces of quiet." Marcus also tried to enhance some of the many activities of his demanding days by relying on his own version of blended or piggybacked reflection. "Dwell on the beauty of life," he told himself, "and watch the stars, and see yourself running with them."[13] Marcus was among the original practitioners of mosaic reflection, and his *Meditations* clearly demonstrate the versatility and power of this approach, particularly for men and women with demanding responsibilities.

## Using Your "Spaces of Quiet"

Suppose you follow some version of the guidance in this chapter. From time to time, you observe yourself. You look for times and places that let you slow down the merry-go-round of life and work and step back, if only briefly and partially, and make your way around whatever obstacles to reflection you face. These are your "spaces of quiet," however brief they might be.

But how do you use them? What do you actually do when you step back? Where do you focus your attention? What should you try to think about? And how can you use these periods of time to move past the obstacles to reflection that you face?

Each of the next three chapters gives a time-tested answer to these questions. Each is basically a different and fundamental way of reflecting. Each has deep roots in the long history of serious thought about reflection. And the interviews confirmed the value of these approaches, because many of the managers were actually following versions of them, even though they were unaware of their origins.

## 3

# Downshift
# Occasionally

A very busy executive, who managed a staff of fifteen hundred people, had an unusual way of creating brief moments of reflection during her workdays. When she had meetings away from her office, she sometimes left early, not to be sure she arrived on time, but just to "make my way there slowly." She wasn't looking for problems or opportunities or trying to "manage by walking around." All she wanted to accomplish, as she put it, was getting a "feel for how things are going."

To my surprise, several other managers defined re- flection in similar terms. One said, "At times I try to be in the moment and not be living in the past and not be projecting the future, but be present to the people or issues or the circumstances in which I'm located." Another added, "I need to put aside time and not try to force things and to be less fevered and just see what comes up." These managers were saying they wanted to liberate themselves, occasionally and briefly, from the focused, analytical, pragmatic way of thinking that they relied on almost automatically.

At work, our minds often resemble race-car engines, tuned to operate at 200 miles an hour. These managers wanted to take a break from this and mentally "downshift." This is a fundamental way of reflecting that, for millennia, has been called *contemplation*—a word that comes from the ancient Roman practice of designating certain areas as *templae*. This is where high priests would patiently and quietly observe natural phenomena in order to discern messages from the gods.[1]

When you downshift or contemplate, you are consciously trying to suspend your default mental habits of analytical thinking, cost-benefit analysis, and planning next steps. Your goal is to simply look around, watch, and observe. Downshifting is a way of really seeing and fully grasping what matters at a meeting, in a conversation, during time with family and friends, or in quiet moments you spend by yourself. It is a form of reflection that helps you be present, alert, and responsive to other people, to situations, to unfolding events. Its basic aim is depth of experience.

Sometimes downshifting matters profoundly. Henry David Thoreau famously lived for two years in an isolated cabin because he "wished to live deliberately, to front only the essential facts of life . . . and not, when I came to die, discover that I had not lived."[2] Michel de Montaigne, the sixteenth-century Frenchman whose *Essays* are a classic work of reflection, had a similar view, but Montaigne focused on enhancing life rather than contemplating death. He wrote, "It is an absolute perfection and almost divine to loyally enjoy our own being."[3]

The fundamental aim of downshifting or contemplation is deepening your sense of what you are experiencing at any point in time. What does this first fundamental type of reflection mean in practical terms? How do you actually go about doing it? And how does it help you overcome the obstacles to reflection? The interviews and the long history suggest four basic ways of downshifting and gaining depth of experience. Each of the four approaches has advantages and drawbacks—which is why you should try each of them and see what works best for you.

## Mental Meandering

The first way of downshifting is letting your mind wander and see where it goes. This means looking up from your screen and taking a brief break from processing task after task and meeting your responsibilities. If this is hard for you, tell yourself that these momentary breaks can lead, as they probably do, to better productivity and effectiveness in the longer run. And with a few minutes of mental meandering and other forms of downshifting, you can even begin to reflect on uncomfortable topics.

For example, one manager said he occasionally went to yoga classes, and an experience at one of them stuck in his mind. For several weeks, he had been dealing with a long series of practical problems that followed his father's recent death. In one class, he found himself watching what he called "a slideshow in my mind."

He saw images of his mother continuing to live in the family home and other images of her in assisted living facilities. He saw his sister, whom he described as a "hot mess," reacting to their father's death and their mother's new circumstances. He saw himself talking to his young daughters about some unspecified but serious concern. This "slideshow" had no voiceover or captions. And he didn't try to make decisions or reach conclusions. All he did was watch the images and memories as they passed through his mind.

Mental meandering can take you in several different directions. You might find yourself simply observing something going on around you, at work or at home. You might surface some questions or concerns that you had pushed aside while you were getting other things done. Sometimes mental meandering involves paying soft, gentle attention to the flow of your feelings—trying, as one manager put it, to get a sense of what was going on "between my belt buckle and my head."

There are no road maps or rules for this way of downshifting. It is spending a few minutes letting your thoughts, feelings, and attention wander where they will. That may sound simple, but actually doing it is a real challenge—particularly for men and women whose minds are trained to process task after task and who feel good being productive. Hence, it takes a focused effort in order to "unfocus."

The interviews suggested several ways of doing this. One manager said that, every weekend, she tried "to do something where my mind is what I will call blank and where I am intentionally not focusing on anything, like sitting in a comfortable chair with a glass of wine or a cup of coffee and doing nothing else." You can also look for particular places that liberate your mind. The Japanese manager who missed his opportunities to bathe while he was in the United States said, "I spend almost all my time kind of planning. So at times I have to experience the bath. There I'm not going to think about anything. I'm just going to enjoy the water, enjoy the quiet."

These examples of downshifting are basically versions of Montaigne's way of reflecting. His diaries were an effort at simple, bare-bones introspection. The literal meaning of introspection is "looking inside," and all Montaigne tried to do was observe and record what was passing through his mind. Mental meandering can trace its roots back even further. This style of reflection originated in the Eastern rather than the Western world, where the earliest followers of the Buddha and Confucius developed a wide range of contemplative practices, all clustered around the single question: What am I experiencing—right now, at this very moment?[4]

What makes mental meandering worthwhile? The answer was sketched early in the last century by an extraordinary Englishman named John Lubbock. He was a London banker, an active member of Parliament, a philanthropist, and an important writer on archaeology and paleontology. Lubbock's life sounds like an unending sequence of demanding, engaging, and important tasks. Yet he wrote, "Rest is not idleness, and to lie sometimes on the grass under trees on a summer's day, listening to the murmur of the water, or watching the clouds float across the sky, is by no means a waste of time."[5]

Lubbock's view has now been confirmed by contemporary studies of our minds. Until about twenty years ago, cognitive neuroscientists thought our brains were idling, like a parked car with its engine running, when we weren't focusing on a task. However, a large body of evidence now indicates that our minds remain active all the time. When we are thinking about doing something and when we are actually doing it, we utilize a particular neural network. But when we stop focusing and doing, another set of circuits lights up. This happens automatically, by default, and hence is called the *default network*.[6]

Recent research on the default network suggests that periods of quiet, contemplative reflection may serve a wide range of purposes. It may be a source of creativity, enable children to engage fully in play, help us with conscious planning for the future, heighten our self-awareness, raise our emotional intelligence, and enhance our moral judgments. There are even indications that the time we spend with our minds "idling" actually improves our conscious, analytical thinking about tasks.

And there may be much deeper rewards: the development of an inner life, as opposed to the productive, active outer life encouraged by society today. The novelist Marilynne Robinson pointed toward the importance of quiet contemplation in her novel *Gilead*, when she wrote, "I know more than I know and must learn it from myself."[7] And Walt Whitman famously said, "I loaf and invite my soul."[8]

Mental meandering, in its various forms, can sound like a fairly straightforward, even easy approach to reflection. All you have to do is follow some version of the venture capitalist's advice to put your feet up and look out the window. But there are three problems with the meandering version of reflection, and each of them can keep you from overcoming the obstacles to reflection.

The first is that some people find it very hard to stop thinking, let their minds go, and passively observe their experience. Following John Lubbock's advice to lie on the grass and listen to the murmur of the water isn't an option for them. As one manager put it, "Sometimes I wish I could shut my brain down and not think about things, but I've never figured out how to shut my brain down." For some people, this is true almost all the time. For others, it is sometimes true and, when it happens, they need other ways to downshift.

The second problem is that paying attention to "the present moment" can be empty advice for some people. In other words, what is it, at any particular moment, that we should pay attention to? The many objects, large and small, in our immediate environment—and which ones? Our physical sensations? To one or several of the feelings and thoughts coursing through our minds? To memories that surface along the way? To the tasks on our to-do list that ping us incessantly? Painters, whose works can look like straightforward representations of reality, actually make a vast array of choices about what to portray and how to portray it.[9] For them and for us, the present moment isn't a single, simple thing.

This is a problem that Montaigne understood fully and described brilliantly. When he reflected, he tried to grasp and portray his immediate experiences, his thoughts, and his feelings, as faithfully as possible. But Montaigne ultimately concluded, "I cannot hold my object still. It keeps shifting and staggering, with a kind of inherent drunkenness . . . I do not portray being. I portray transition."[10]

The final problem is rumination. When this happens, your thoughts return, again and again, to the same incident, problem, or concern.[11] Rumination is like a piece of music you can't get out of your head. One manager said that, when she tried to sit quietly, her mind often kept circling and coming back to "something I'd screwed up or some relationship where there was disagreement or anger."

In short, mental meandering isn't for everyone. But, fortunately, there are other ways of downshifting. They all involve focusing your attention in a soft, gentle, open-ended way. All of them are ways of seeking depth of experience, for a few moments or longer. Like mosaic tiles, you can combine them in different ways, over the course of a day or a week, depending on your needs, inclinations, and the time you have available.

## Slow Down

One manager apologized for one of his views of reflection, because he thought it might sound corny. From time to time, he said, either he or his wife would notice something, like one of their children being especially kind, and say to the other, "Behold." They did this to slow down occasionally and really experience something. They were trying to push aside the screen of thoughts, feelings, and categories through which we usually filter and interpret reality to create a moment of deeper experience.

Quakers do something like this when they sit in silence as part of their worship. As one theologian put it, it "makes possible a way of seeing that takes us beyond the limits of words."[12] This approach to downshifting is easy to understand and easy to do, because you can do it in an unlimited range of ways. The basic idea is to notice something you are doing, consciously do it more slowly, and simply see what you experience.

Thoughtful journals and diaries give us clear examples of this approach. They show us men and women trying to simply capture and relive an experience—without analyzing it or drawing lessons from it. And the very act of keeping a diary—taking time, sitting down, and writing something out by hand—is an exercise in slowness.

One of the notable diarists of the twentieth century is a little-known but extraordinarily successful executive named David Lilienthal. During the 1930s, he directed the creation of the Tennessee Valley Authority, a vast, multistate complex of hydroelectric facilities. During the 1940s, Lilienthal was the founding head of the Atomic Energy Commission, at a time when the new technology of nuclear power promised to radically enhance or eradicate human life. During the 1950s, he founded and ran an international consulting firm, advising on large-scale government projects in the developing world.

Despite these responsibilities, Lilienthal found time to record his reflections in what ultimately became six lengthy volumes. Many of his entries simply record events, some significant, and some minor or amusing. One entry, for example, describes how Lilienthal rode to a dam site in Iran with the country's minister of agriculture and two American oil executives. All three were wearing heavy sunglasses and large, earmuff-like devices to dampen the noise. Lilienthal writes that, at one point, he saw their reflection in the window, and they reminded him of the three monkeys who "hear no evil, see no evil, speak no evil."[13]

In these passages, Lilienthal was simply describing an experience, almost as if he was trying to relive it and enjoy it once again. This was downshifting in the spirit of the writer Anaïs Nin, who observed, "We write to taste life twice, in the moment and in retrospect."[14] Many famous diaries have long stretches of similar entries. Anne Frank, for example, often recounts minor details of her family's life in hiding from the Nazis, which seem utterly inconsequential when set against the horrific circumstances through which they were living.[15]

Lilienthal and Frank, along with many other diarists, are descendants of Samuel Pepys, the seventeenth-century London government official whose extraordinarily varied observations are widely viewed as the first modern diary. Page after page of his journal simply describe the comings and goings of his everyday life with a gusto and charm—and sometimes with a startling candor; for example, about illicit affairs and personal habits—that continue to captivate readers.

How do you find your way of "beholding?" One answer is slowing down occasionally and keeping a journal of some kind, as roughly one in five of the managers did or tried to do. Other approaches are variations of the senior manager's tactic of walking slowly to some of her meetings. The basic idea is to find your own ways to slow down, if only for a few brief moments. This usually means slowing down physically in order to slow down mentally—the equivalent of turning the dial on an old-fashioned radio very slowly to tune in a distant signal.

Marcel Proust, the early-twentieth-century French novelist, is famous for his seven-volume masterwork, *In Search of Lost Time*. Long stretches of these novels are extraordinarily attentive contemplations of individual moments. They also illustrate a bit of Proust's advice on living well. "N'allez pas trop vite," he once said. That is, "Don't go too fast."[16] This guidance recurs through much of the long history. In earlier eras, a slower pace of life probably made it easier to do this, but even Montaigne, living in rural France more than four centuries ago, wrote, "Experience has taught me this, that we destroy ourselves by our own impatience."[17]

This is why some of the managers found a variety of ways to slow themselves down during their hurried days—in the hopes that occasionally and briefly changing what they did physically would help them experience and observe what was going on in their offices, factories, homes, and neighborhoods. As one manager put it, "My goal in life is to figure out on a daily basis how to slow down and to slow myself down."

## Turning to Nature

Few of the managers were "rugged outdoor" types, but several defined reflection as quietly observing and experiencing nature in one way or another. In doing this, they were practicing a version of reflection that runs through the long history and is available to almost everyone today. It is also a way of freeing up your mind for a few moments but with less risk of rumination and the other problems of simple mental meandering.

It isn't surprising that the experience of nature can put you in a contemplative frame of mind. Psychologists, biologists, and naturalists use the word *biophilia* to describe this phenomenon. Our ancient ancestors lived and evolved in close proximity to nature and probably passed down to us an innate inclination to experience nature and other forms of life.[18] This, for example, may explain why pets enhance the lives and health of many people and why hospital patients who can see out windows may recover more quickly.[19]

You can turn to nature in a wide variety of ways, and none of them requires a day of hiking in the woods. A very simple option is taking a moment or two as a break in the flow of work, and looking at a beautiful outdoor photo on a computer or an indoor plant or a print on the wall. One manager said that, from time to time, she got up from her desk and walked over to a window and spent a moment or two looking at a small, nearby tree. Some of the managers made an effort to take short walks outside during their workdays. And one tried to spend a little while on most nights in his hot tub. He especially liked watching satellites move across the stars, because his father was one of the first American astronauts.

Turning to nature can sound easy, but it isn't—especially when you feel you should really be keeping your nose to the grindstone. One manager quoted her father, a farmer, as saying, "The number of people who can walk outside and just look up is so small." This kind of downshifting usually takes a little time and effort, and may need tentative scheduling. Two managers said that, on weekends, they made a point of simply sitting outside with a cup of coffee or a glass of wine. Others made a conscious effort to take occasional walks, and one said, "I golf, and I'm out there by myself, and in the summer you can get out at 5:00 or 5:30 and it's a very contemplative thing, a kind of Zen."

But are these simple experiences of nature actually reflection? Or are they merely pleasant ways to spend time? The answer to these questions is no, and a brief look at the long history makes this clear. For example, the *Spiritual Exercises* of Ignatius Loyola reflect his early years as a soldier. They present a rigorous, detailed, comprehensive plan for four weeks of spiritual practices. Yet one of Ignatius's biographers noted that, "The greatest consolation he received was from gazing at the sky and the stars and the sea. He did this often and sometimes for quite a long time."[20] The Jesuit poet Gerard Manley Hopkins distilled Ignatius's broader perspective when he wrote, "The world is charged with the grandeur of God."[21]

Marcus Aurelius—a no-nonsense, practical man of action—spent some of his few free moments in simple contemplation of the natural world and gained a deeper understanding of himself.[22] In *Meditations*, Marcus often expresses his awe at the cosmos and reflects, "Remember how small a part you are of universal nature; how small a moment of the whole duration is appointed for you."[23]

## Celebrate

An unusual approach to reflection appeared in roughly ten of the interviews, and one former manager spoke about its importance with real urgency. He insisted that men and women today need ways to escape what he called the "psychic prison of continuous improvement." This was a reference to the Japanese practice of *kaizen*, whose basic idea is a never-ending and endless search for improved performance. He believed this was an important management technique and also a disturbing prescription for a relentless, joyless approach to work and life, governed by the principle "Strive, strive, strive."

The manager's antidote, for himself and the people he worked with, was to occasionally make time for celebration. "You can celebrate lots of things," he said. "Celebrate the number of happy customers. Or just say "This is what we managed to achieve, and it's really good." As he saw it, celebration was simply paying attention to something that had gone well and enjoying the experience. It didn't involve personal self-improvement. It didn't involve analyzing what led to the success or planning next steps. For a work group, he said, celebration was, "Just rubbing the certificate and saying, 'Gee, we did this.'" For an individual, it was thinking, "Look what it was like before I did this and look what I've accomplished."

Another manager—an extremely well-organized and productive individual—endorsed celebration and put it in a religious context. He said, "I think the Mormon tradition is that life is hard and often painful, and so we have to appreciate our blessings, and I think that is what I'm preaching to you now." Then he smiled and added, "When I start my own church, it's going to be about this appreciation for our blessings, end of story, end of story."

Celebration may not sound like reflection, because we tend to think that reflection is a serious business, typically focused on momentous questions and somber aspects of life. Eighteenth-century Scotsman James Boswell wrote a famous biography of his good friend, the British literary giant Samuel Johnson, and one passage emphasizes the tension between reflecting seriously on life and celebrating it. Boswell quotes one of Johnson's old friends saying, "You are a philosopher, Dr. Johnson. I have tried too in my time to be a philosopher; but, I don't know how, cheerfulness was always breaking in."[24]

Our minds may naturally turn away from "cheerfulness" and home in on problems, threats, and difficulties and to ways of dealing with them—because this instinct may have helped our species survive. Montaigne had this tendency when he referred to our "killjoy, sickly minds."[25] Psychologists now call this *asymmetric negative bias*.[26] This tendency may disproportionately describe hardworking, successful people who often feel they are falling short of the high standards they set for themselves and failing to appreciate all they are doing and have done. This is why the psychoanalyst Adam Phillips wrote recently, "We have to imagine a world in which celebration is less suspect than criticism."[27]

The interviews provided a wide range of brief, useful, everyday ways to downshift and celebrate—along with an important, overall guideline. Celebration doesn't mean partying or festivities and can simply be a moment of quiet appreciation. For example, one manager described a college reunion this way: "We weren't just sitting around talking about how we've done. Content really didn't matter. What mattered was just knowing there was a backwards and a past that we really valued. My past was just there. There was a kind of peace. It was really satisfying."

Another manager said that, on Sunday evenings, before he and his wife went to bed, "We typically spend ten minutes before bed recounting the last two days and maybe looking at each other's photos of a few funny moments from the prior forty-eight hours. It's not much, but it's enough to feel satisfied and blessed."

The interviews also suggest that you can look for ways to weave moments of celebration into the tasks of the day. One manager, for example, described rereading his father's will to prepare for a meeting with a lawyer, and found himself noticing how carefully and thoughtfully his father had allocated the small amounts he was leaving to grandchildren and a few friends. This, in turn, reminded him of his father's generosity, not with money but with his time and attention. This "reflection" may have taken a minute or two, but it transformed what might have been a mechanical or analytical exercise into a valuable human moment.

For several of the managers who were religious, brief prayers were a way of feeling appreciation and gratitude. For example, one woman whose religion, she said, was "absolutely minimalist" and consisted of an occasional, short prayer, told me, "I think it's more important to say thank you, thank you, thank you for my son Todd and thank you for the opportunities I've had." A retired HR manager said that he "wrote a letter of gratitude once a week, and once again this involved my praying, and I try to make sure God knows what I'm grateful for." A younger manager, a devout practitioner of his faith, said simply, "You address God, and you say what you're thankful for."

Another set of everyday approaches involved different forms of writing. One manager said, "I actually have a journal that my coach provided and part of it is a discipline of writing down in terms of gratitude, and saying what I'm grateful for." The young manager, who followed an approach called "bullet journaling," which is a sharply focused and highly time-efficient way of keeping a diary, said, "Every day, I try to write down something that I'm grateful for, whether it's like something that happened, or a person, or chocolate, or whatever, just to remind myself to be present in life and also to be thankful for things."

Another simple, written tactic is recommended by Marc Andreessen, who helped create Mosaic, the first widely used web browser, and now runs an important venture capital firm in Silicon Valley. Andreessen keeps an "anti-to-do list." This is a running list of everything he does during the day. It gives him, he says, a sense of accomplishment, a feeling of confidence, and motivation to continue working through the many tasks and challenges of his days.[28]

Finally, if more serious journal keeping seems worthwhile to you, you can experiment with a range of approaches and customize one for yourself. For example, one manager kept two sets of journals and wrote in each of them from time to time. One was for planning what she wanted to accomplish over the next several months. The other was her own version of a "bucket list"—but this wasn't a list of places to go and things to do before she died. Her list was for looking back and capturing moments that she wanted to recall and re-experience. As she put it:

These are the moments that meant something to me. This was something so extraordinary that I really did feel a need to put down, you know, to remember things that you couldn't believe and you want to remember that feeling you had. Like your kid's first birthday and they put their face in the cake. It's not the moment when you press the buzzer at the New York Stock Exchange. It's the morning you woke up and it was snowing and you had nothing to do and you felt like the happiest person in the world. These are pinch-yourself moments.

In short, celebration can take many different forms. As before, what matters is experimenting and looking for approaches you can weave into your daily life.

## Don't Just Do Something

There are many ways to downshift and contemplate for a few moments, but they are all variations on the same basic theme. In the Disney version of *Alice in Wonderland*, the White Rabbit, a chronically late and distracted creature, gives Alice advice that he needs to follow himself. "Don't just do something," he says. "Stand there."[29]

Doing this sounds simple, but you have to observe yourself to find the times and places when you can actually decelerate for a while. A little voice regularly tells us we shouldn't waste time and, if we do pause for a moment, we can hear our mental engines revving in the background. But giving in to this pressure comes at a price. We miss out on depth of experience. Over time, we end up managing and processing our lives rather than living them.

Meandering, slowing down, experiencing nature, and celebrating can filter out some of the stimuli that constantly bombard us. They are fundamentally ways to gain depth of experience and keep too much of your life from going by in a highly productive blur. At one point, believing the end of his life was the new year, Montaigne wrote, "I try to increase it in weight, I try to arrest the speed of its flight by the speed with which I grasp it . . . The shorter my possession of life, the deeper and fuller I must make it."[30]

But doing this is a challenge and takes effort. In *The Art of Stillness*, the essayist Pico Iyer writes, "It takes courage, of course, to step out of the fray."[31] It also takes close attention because you need to find ways of weaving contemplative pauses into your actual, everyday life and do this in a way that you can sustain, on a "good enough" basis, over the longer run. The most effective approaches are ones that you enjoy doing, because this can temporarily lower the obstacles to reflection.

Moments of quiet contemplation are important in their own right, but they are important in another way. By quieting our minds to some degree, these reflective pauses can clear the way for another important form of reflection, one that can help us make progress on the really hard problems of work and life.

# 4

# Ponder the Tough Issues

Almost everyone knows a few people who are especially good at thinking through problems and understanding complicated situations. What sets them apart, quite often, is their skill at a fundamental type of reflection, best described as *pondering*. It opens the door to deeper understanding, insight, and creativity and better decisions—on personal and professional issues.

What is pondering? Here is a clear example, taken from an interview with a manager who was seriously considering a new professional opportunity. To preserve confidentiality, we will call him Mateo. He had spent the first fifteen years of his career working in New York for a financial firm. Then he made a radical career change and began working as the senior financial officer at a major hospital, so he could travel less and have more family time. Mateo had recently been asked about going to work as a senior adviser to the Ministry of Finance in the South American country where he had been born and raised and where his elderly father lived.

This is how Mateo described one of the times when he reflected on what to do:

I had the plane ride back, which, as we both know, is a moment for reflection because you're not distracted by other things and actually you can step back into yourself.

. . . I needed more information—what is this office, where I would work, and what does it do? So there is a chunk of due diligence that I had to do. And then it's a technical job, but it's in the fluid world of politics, so what does that mean? Governments go and governments come. Would I even be good at this, and would it be something I would be excited about doing? Then there's a whole lifestyle perspective. Do I want to get back into being in meetings all day long? It's an exciting job and it would be energizing and I would have a direct line to the prime minister, but then you have to put in the balance what you already have versus what you would gain, and sometimes the ultimate needle goes back and forth. So I started reflecting on my life here. And the truth is I love it here. I love what I do, and I think I'm getting better and better at what I do, and I'm contributing to the place and I've learned a lot, and I've grown intellectually. And it's been a wonderful personal experience, and now with my kids going to college, I could devote myself even more to this job.

. . . And at the same time, there's the longer-range plan, which is you're not getting any younger, so what are you going to do when you grow up? I also think there's a nobility in this new job. And a very big thing is that my father is ninety years old and lives where I would be working and so I think, maybe, how much time does he really have, and should I be closer to him?

To understand what pondering is, notice what Mateo didn't do. He wasn't trying to analyze his situation, find the right answer, or make a decision. Instead, he was thinking about his decision in a flexible, open-ended way by examining it from a wide range of perspectives. Depending on how you count, Mateo was looking at his decision from five or perhaps ten different angles, and he was also noticing how he felt about each of these perspectives.

This is the essence of pondering. It is trying to grasp what really matters about an issue or a problem by coming back to it again and again and looking at it from a variety of angles. Pondering supposes that hard issues have different facets and angles, and each is worth at least some consideration. Hence, instead of making quick judgments, you are sifting through a range of possibilities and seeing what you can learn. Pondering relies on what the poet John Keats called "negative capability"—that is, the skill of "being in uncertainties, mysteries, doubts, without any irritable reaching after fact and reason."[1]

Looking at a problem or a question from different perspectives may sound easy, but it isn't. We often respond to complex situations with quick, instinctive, definitive reactions or answers. Even worse, we often stick like glue to our initial positions. And these aren't just bad habits—we seem to be hardwired to behave this way. A recent book, *Thinking, Fast and Slow* by Daniel Kahneman, presents a vast range of experiments and real-world examples showing that we are spring-loaded to produce fast and firm convictions on a wide range of topics and questions.[2] "Slow" thinking, which is akin to pondering, is our biological and evolutionary exception, not the Darwinian rule.

Many of the managers seemed to understand the importance of pondering and the difficulty of doing it, and they had improvised a variety of ways to broaden and shift their perspectives. Many of the important figures in the long history also developed ways of dealing with this problem. The interviews and the classics give us five basic strategies for pondering a problem or an issue and gaining depth of understanding.

## Shift Your Mindset

If you want to spend time pondering, the first important step is shifting your mindset. Rigorous, analytical, problem-solving thinking is often indispensable, and we probably don't rely on it often enough, but it is the enemy of pondering, which requires a loose, modest, curious, even playful frame of mind.

The best way to see what this means in practice is a brief look at one of the most important classic works of reflection, Michel de Montaigne's *Essays*. Montaigne lived during the sixteenth century in the southwest of France. He "retired" at the age of forty, believing his life was nearing its end, but he lived another thirty years. During these years, Montaigne managed his large family vineyard, served two terms as mayor of Bordeaux, and occasionally performed diplomatic missions for the king of France, at a time of deep religious divisions in the country and frequent outbreaks of religious violence.[3] Despite an active life and turbulent times, Montaigne composed his *Essays*, a masterpiece of introspection and reflection.

The *Essays* are "reflection" in its most literal sense. Montaigne wanted his writing to mirror whatever impressions, thoughts, and feelings were passing through his mind, whether he was writing about inconsequential, everyday aggravations or profound aspects of life. Montaigne rarely declared that he had found "the truth" about a problem or a topic. Instead he advocated modesty, writing:

> Presumption is our natural and original disease.
> The most wretched and frail of all creatures is
> man, and withal the proudest. He feels and sees
> himself lodged here in the dirt and filth of the
> world . . . and yet in his imagination will be plac-

ing himself above the circle of the moon, and bringing the heavens under his feet.[4]

Montaigne's modesty was displayed on a small medallion he is believed to have worn around his neck. It was inscribed with the question, "Que sais je?" or "What do I know?"[5]

Yet, unlike some skeptics, who want to obliterate any possible knowledge, Montaigne was endlessly curious. He studied and reflected on a vast range of topics, and you can see them in the titles of his essays. These include "Of Thumbs," "On Cannibals," "Of Experience," "Of Coaches," "Of Cruelty," and "Of the Custom of Wearing Clothes." In some of these essays, Montaigne's curiosity and modesty were matched with playfulness as he toyed with new perspectives on a topic. In one essay, he muses on the inner life of animals and asks, "When I play with my cat, who knows if I am not a pastime to her more than she is to me?"[6]

Many of the great diaries reveal similar mindsets. Anne Frank's diaries lack the charm and playfulness of some of Montaigne's essays—which is hardly surprising given the grim and dangerous ordeal she and her family were enduring—but her entries often describe the inconsequential behavior of family members and her reactions to it. Frank is trying to understand them better by reflecting briefly on different aspects of their personalities. David Lilienthal followed a similar approach. Many of his diary entries consist of a few lines describing a person, a meeting, or an event. He spends just a few minutes looking at it from different angles and then moves on.

How do you shift your mindset? One manager did this in a distinctive way that dramatizes two broad, practical lessons. He kept a whiteboard in his office. When he really wanted to think something through, he got up from his desk, walked around the office, picked up several colored markers, and then "doodled" on the whiteboard, drawing simple diagrams and writing a few words, and then he walked around a little more.

The first lesson is the importance of stepping back, mentally and physically. By getting up from his desk, moving away from his computer screen, and writing on the whiteboard, he was following his version of the advice a venture capitalist gave to CEOs—to put up their feet and look out the window—so they wouldn't spend all their time "putting out fires." Shifting your mindset seems to require shifting your body.

The second lesson involves "doodling." This manager wasn't focused on finding the right answer or completing a rigorous analysis. He was toying with his issue, drawing pictures and using various colors. This was his way of briefly getting past a major obstacle to reflection—the cult of productivity, with its focus on the relentless and efficient processing of task after task. Another manager did something similar on paper. He wrote "almost indecipherable notes and primitive pictures" that "represented whatever was going through my mind." Without knowing it, both managers were following Albert Einstein's observation that, "to stimulate creativity, one must develop the childlike inclination for play."

When Montaigne entitled his masterwork *Essays*, he was using the word in its contemporary, sixteenth-century sense. For him, "essays" were tests and trials, not short pieces of expository writing. They were his way of fighting a common human tendency that he described when he wrote, "We are all huddled and concentrated in ourselves, and our vision is reduced to the length of our noses."[7] On topic after topic, Montaigne tested a wide range of ideas to see what he could learn from them and to grasp their full complexity. Pondering is a version of this kind of reflection. It is treating an issue or a situation as an image in a kaleidoscope and then twisting the tube and seeing what you can learn from new patterns and combinations.

## Rely on Anchoring Questions

In some ways, pondering resembles a solar system. At its center is a question or concern, like the question of whether Mateo should take the new job. A variety of thoughts, feelings, intuitions, and impressions orbit around it. The gravitational pull of the central question or concern should keep your thoughts from drifting away. But actually doing this can be difficult because, when you want to ponder a question or an issue, you face two challenges.

One is staying focused on whatever question or issue you want to really think through. You want to let your mind range widely in order to find new perspectives, but the risk is that something comes along—a striking impression, a compelling idea, or a strong feeling—and hijacks your attention. This is the obstacle to all reflection that originates in our restless, zigzagging minds. The other challenge can be generating new perspectives, because our thoughts and feelings often run in well-worn grooves and ruts.

One way to deal with both problems is by asking yourself one of several questions and spending a few minutes answering it. These questions are mental anchors that help you stay focused on your central concern while, at the same time, expanding your perspectives.

For example, you can ask yourself to imagine—in a vivid, concrete, visual way—the important aspects of whatever you are pondering. Mateo did this when he considered the new position. As he put it:

This wasn't just analytical thinking. Oh no, totally, totally I was projecting myself into the new position. So one example is that I started to look at real estate in the capital, and I asked what could I afford.

. . . What it does is make it real. You start thinking about how you would spend weekends and the people you would meet, the food, the lifestyle, everything. It's like watching a little video in your mind and deciding, "I'd like to do this but I wouldn't like to do that."

By painting an image of the lived details of a possible future life, Mateo was utilizing a technique for reflection that is centuries old and probably has an evolutionary origin. We have survived as a species because we can think, and this is why we are called *homo sapiens*. But we are also *homo prospectus*. We imagine possible futures and take them into account when we make decisions.[8]

These mental videos can elicit new reactions, thoughts, and feelings, which deepens our understanding of situations and problems.

Another anchoring question asks if there are certain perspectives—and, in particular, certain feelings—you are trying to avoid. This question is a way of tackling one of the major obstacles to reflection: an intuitive reluctance to look in certain directions because this might surface uncomfortable thoughts and feelings. As one manager put it:

> Sometimes I can just sense like I'm missing something or there's an element that I haven't picked up on, or don't want to pick up on, or just a big piece of information that I don't know yet. My thinking just feels shallow. I'm like the spider who has its legs out on the web and I'm trying to see where the fly is and waiting for that little string to quiver.

In Mateo's case, those feelings centered on the fact that his father was quite elderly. Thoughts about his father's mortality, and possibly his own, lingered on the outskirts of Mateo's consciousness.

A good way to see these largely submerged, but partly visible concerns is to step back, downshift for a few moments in some way you find comfortable, and try to let your feelings emerge. As one manager put it, "A lot of reflection is listening to your feelings and accepting them, whatever they are. I think that very often we are too much focused or I am too much focused on logic and what my head is doing."

Another valuable anchoring question is asking how someone you really respect would think and feel about the problem or situation you are pondering. Several managers said their parents played this role. Others imagined the reactions of leaders they admired, and several relied on a religious or spiritual figure to give them a valuable perspective on an issue.

Bracelets with the letters "WWJD" or "What would Jesus do?" are version of this anchoring question. These bracelets have been parodied—for example, by replacing "Jesus" with the name of a celebrity or a notorious criminal—but many important figures in the long history relied on versions of this approach. When he reflected, Marcus Aurelius sometimes turned to the views of the Stoic philosopher Epictetus. Montaigne relied at times on his father's thoughts and example and on important writers in ancient Greece and Rome whose works he knew intimately.

Another version of this question is trying to discern the perspective of your future self. As Mateo put it, "You have to think, at some point, about legacy. What if you went tomorrow? What would people say about you?" The optimistic version of this question asks you to view an issue from the perspective of your abiding aspirations and standards. The alternative is Mateo's somber approach. He asks about legacy, but in the context of his own death. Both versions of this anchoring question can shift your perspective from a preoccupation with output and productivity to your deeper, long-term concerns.

## Talk with Yourself

Several managers pondered tough issues in a remarkable way. One said, "I absolutely talk to myself, and sometimes I can even see my brow furrowing while I do it." Another said, "Some of my best conversations are with myself." This approach can sound eccentric, and is best done in private, but it has an impressive lineage.

If we search the Western tradition for the earliest and most influential example of serious deliberation, we find the Socratic dialogue. This is a flowing, back-and-forth exchange of questions and perspectives on the most serious topics of politics, knowledge, and life. It is a model—perhaps *the* model—for pursuing deeper understanding by multiplying and examining a series of perspectives on complicated, important issues.

Every few pages in the *Meditations*, we find Marcus Aurelius talking to himself, in the form of observations and admonitions that he explicitly addresses to himself, just as some of the managers did. Some scholars speculate that, at certain points in *Meditations*, Marcus was actually talking with another person or was vividly imagining one.[9]

In many religious traditions, prayer takes the form of a conversation with God. Several managers said they "talked with themselves" when they prayed. They meant they were speaking to God and believed that God sometimes replied to them, not through spoken words, but by conveying a strong sense of what was right or important. A Jesuit scholar summarized his order's approach by writing, "We have a personal relationship with God. Prayer in the Ignatian mode is essentially a conversation."[10]

The interviews indicated several ways to have conversations with yourself. And you can do each of them as a way of explicitly structuring your thinking, even if you don't say any words aloud. One is trying to state your thoughts or feelings in a few words or a sentence or two. One manager said her conversations with herself, "force me to be precise about what I'm really worried about." The aim is distilling the essence of the essence.

Another approach is to structure a debate in your head. One manager said, "You know the old pictures of left shoulder and right shoulder, I can do the entire discussion and debate in my head, over and over again, and maybe then on a piece of paper."

Other approaches are more open-ended. One manager said:

> I mentioned that I rely on questions. It's usually a series of questions, and as I'm trying to answer the first one or think I'm close to it, then the second one usually comes up, and I try to answer that. So what's happening is that part of my mind is kind of questioning another part of my mind, really explicitly.

And another is to develop your own customized questions and then "talk with yourself" and develop answers to them. One manager described this approach by saying:

> With different problems, what I try to do is ask: "Have I faced this in the past? What did I do? How did it work? Was it successful the way I did it in the

past or should we go about it in a different way?"
There are very few new problems around here.

Pausing and having a brief conversation with yourself is another way to break away from our productivity and output mentality. Like the other ways of pondering, it can help you understand a tough problem more deeply and keep you from missing an important perspective on it.

## Live with Your Question

This is another surprising way of pondering. Sometimes, a good way to reflect on an issue is to stop reflecting on it. The idea is to live with your issue by putting it on the back burner, coming back to it occasionally, and seeing if you have a new way of thinking about it.

What does this mean in practice? The former CEO of a major American retailer answered this question clearly:

With challenging decisions, I carry them with me throughout the day. I don't think you sit down at a desk and say, "Now I'm going to decide on X." It may be unconscious how my thought process is working, but it's very conscious that I am

deliberately carrying it with me and coming back
to it from time to time and not letting it go.

This executive was talking about major business decisions. He said he sometimes lived with them for days or
longer—particularly if they involved large investments
or shifts in strategy. But this approach is surprising in a
second way; it echoes a theme running through the literature on contemplative religious lives. Thomas Merton,
the theologian and Trappist monk, observed, "One of
the strange laws of the contemplative life is that in it you
do not sit down and solve problems: you bear with them
until they somehow solve themselves."[11]

What makes living with an issue or problem a particularly valuable way of pondering? The former CEO
pointed to an important explanation when he mentioned
his unconscious mind. We usually assume that thinking
is a conscious activity. If someone asks us what we are
thinking about, we can usually tell them. But we also
think unconsciously.

In a recent book, *Strangers to Ourselves*, the social psychologist Timothy Wilson summarizes recent findings in
psychology and cognitive neuroscience and concludes that
each of us is equipped with an "adaptive unconscious."[12]
Wilson isn't referring to Sigmund Freud's unconscious

mind, which was a cauldron of primeval drives and desires. The adaptive unconscious does something akin to thinking. Outside our awareness, like a computer operating system, it observes, assesses, and even makes judgments.

These findings from contemporary neuroscience confirm the prescient observation of Blaise Pascal, the brilliant seventeenth-century French mathematician, physicist, and theologian. Pascal wrote, "The heart has its reasons that reason does not know."[13] One manager described her version of this experience by saying:

You're not being influenced by very smart people with persuasive facts and logic trying to convince you. You're letting reflection bring together your instincts, the facts, your values, and then producing a certain output, maybe when you wake up or get back to the problem. It may not be the second day. It may be the third day and so forth.

Some of the managers said they relied on specific tactics to harvest the perspectives of their unconscious minds. The former retailing executive said:

If something's not coming to my mind or I'm stuck, I'll go onto YouTube and watch the great

video about top Tony Award moments on Broad-
way. It'll be Idina Menzel singing "Defying Grav-
ity." It'll be Mandy Gonzalez singing something
from *In the Heights*. It'll be whatever.

Mateo tried to "sleep on" difficult issues. He said, "I
think this is just a human thing. When I have a big problem that I'm dealing with here at work or something
like that, it's always better to sleep on it." He emphasized
this approach by mentioning a proverb from his home
country: "Sleep is a counselor."

Another practical approach is putting a time limit on
your conscious reflection on an issue or a problem and
then putting it aside and doing something else. This
is a way of avoiding time-consuming, futile rumination on a problem. Many serious accounts of creativity
describe a common pattern among mathematicians,
scientists, writers, artists, engineers, and others who
achieve important breakthroughs. They work hard on
a problem, but reach a point where they feel frustrated
or blocked. So they shift gears and do something else.
When they return to their problem, they sometimes
find a way forward. And sometimes a fresh perspective
pops into their heads while they are otherwise occupied.
Albert Einstein, for example, is said to have conceived

important elements of his theory of relativity while riding a bicycle.[14]

You can also live with an issue as a way of reflecting on the past and developing fresh perspectives on it. One manager, who had been fired from an important job, said he often came back to certain questions: "What really happened? What could I have done differently to keep the job? And am I still doing whatever led to problems before?"

All of these approaches are ways of shifting your mental apparatus from analysis to pondering. Analytical thinking is a laser. It focuses, sharpens, and concentrates our thinking. In contrast, pondering is carrying a lantern along a dark path. It illuminates broadly but dimly and creates shifting patterns and impressions. This approach can be particularly valuable when you are pondering a serious issue of life and coming back to it, sometimes briefly and sometimes at greater length, over months or years. As time passes and your life experience grows, new perspectives can emerge, even on long-standing questions and concerns.

For example, in the book *God, Faith, and Identity from the Ashes*, the children and grandchildren of Holocaust survivors recount how, sometimes throughout their entire adult lives, they struggled to reconcile faith in God or some semblance of respect for humanity with the vast, incomprehensible evil and suffering of the Holocaust.[15] These are examples of reflection as extended, deeply personal pondering: a search for sound perspectives, unwarped by logical analysis or expectations of linear progress, full clarity, or closure. One woman said that she sometimes thought she had reconciled the Holocaust with her faith, but then, "a week or a month or two later, in a solitary moment, I would cry for the pain of my people. It was my people, my family, my friends, my pain. I asked no questions. I believed in the Almighty. Yet I cried."[16]

Living with an issue requires a sensitive alertness. You are listening for faint, wispy signals—just as scientists use finely calibrated instruments to scan the universe for extraterrestrial life. In *The Art of Reflection: Buddhist Wisdom in Practice*, Ratnaguna Hennessy, a British teacher of Buddhism, writes, "When a thought occurs to me that seems worth following I then exert a gentle effort to stay with it. Just the right amount of effort needed to dwell on that thought to see where it might lead me—I don't need to do any more than that."[17] This is a way of amplifying important, but barely audible voices inside our minds and gaining fresh perspectives on hard issues.

The mosaic approach to reflection can help you live with an issue and gradually make progress on it. You can try to notice new perspectives that occur to you from time to time, seemingly out of the clear blue sky, and then spend a little time seeing what you can learn from them. You can also notice how often an issue returns to your mind, which may indicate its importance to you. Also, momentary intrusions of uncomfortable issues—like Mateo's thoughts about his age and his father—can be small steps toward addressing these issues head-on.

## Beyond Pondering

Marcel Proust wrote that the true art of discovery wasn't discovering new lands, but seeing with new eyes, and this is a good description of the central aim of pondering.[18] It is searching for new perspectives on problems and issues.

Sometimes pondering is worth doing in and of itself. Whether you do it for just a few minutes or for longer, it can help you deepen your understanding of a problem or a difficult situation, at home or at work. But men and women with serious, complicated responsibilities often need to do more than ponder and understand.

Suppose, for example, that you have spent some time pondering a difficult issue. You have tried to look at it in a loose, relaxed, inquiring, and even somewhat playful way. You have asked yourself some anchoring questions to steady but broaden your search for new perspectives. You have talked about the issue in a reflective conversation with someone else or even with yourself. And you have lived with the question for several hours, several days, or even longer and looked for faint intimations from your unconscious mind.

Twisting the kaleidoscope and looking for new patterns and perspectives is valuable but—if you have serious responsibilities in life—it often isn't enough. Sometimes you need to do more than understand deeply. You have to decide, act, and lead. When this is the case, you have to rely on the third, fundamental approach to reflection.

# 5

# Pause and Measure Up

One of the managers was white, male, American, about sixty-five years old, and strongly committed to his church and his religious beliefs. Another was roughly forty years old, female, Indian, and not religious. Despite these dramatically different backgrounds, they had almost identical views of reflection and explained their thinking in the same clear, simple, pragmatic way.

The older manager defined reflection by saying, "The first question is 'What am I doing that I should stop doing?' The second is 'What am I not doing that I should start doing?'" The younger manager said, "I think, to me, reflection is taking time to think through what I have been doing, but also to think about what I'd like to be doing."

These views of reflection have two strong similarities. One is clear: both emphasize "doing." Each uses this word twice in the space of just a few words. The other similarity was beneath the surface and explains the common focus on action. At one point, the older manager paused for a long moment and then said emphatically, "Those are really, really profound questions." The younger manager didn't use the same words, but her interview made clear that she agreed.

Reflection focused on what we decide and do is the third fundamental approach to reflection, and perhaps the most important. The Scottish essayist Thomas Carlyle wrote, "Conviction, were it ever so excellent, is worthless till it converts itself into conduct."[1] We spend our days and our lives deciding and doing. It is how we get our jobs done, take care of ourselves and others, and make a difference in the world.

Grasping what really matters about what we decide and do means answering two questions. Both are serious and sometimes profound. The first asks: Are my decisions and actions measuring up to the standards I have for myself and the standards others expect me to meet?

The second question focuses on the longer-term impact of what we do. It asks: As I make decisions and act over the course of days, weeks, and longer periods of time, am I becoming the kind of person I want to become?

Our actions and our identities are braided together, like the strands of the famous DNA molecule. As one manager put it, when he gave his reason for the importance of reflection, "If you don't do this, life will just intrude in myriad ways, and you'll wake up one day, and you won't have become the person you want to be, and you won't have done what you want to do."

## Measuring without a Yardstick

Sometimes measuring up isn't a challenge. With routine activities, for example, we know what needs to be done and how to do it. In other cases, there are bright lines that tell us how to behave: stealing is wrong so we shouldn't steal. And sometimes you can measure progress. If you want to run a 5K race, you can create a training schedule and monitor your progress. In short, when we have a yardstick of some kind, measuring up isn't a problem.

Unfortunately, this isn't the case for the hard questions of work and life. You might think that measuring up is largely a matter of committing yourself to some basic values or principles and then using them as a yardstick. The problem is that lofty principles and aspirations float far above the complexity and messiness of decisions and actions. They can be the equivalent of trying to save someone struggling in the water twenty feet below a pier by lowering five feet of beautifully woven rope.

One manager pointed to this challenge in his personal definition of reflection:

> Reflection is an image that you see of yourself and it makes you happy. It gives you the satisfaction that you have not just taken from the world but you've given something back. As human beings, it's very easy for us to just take. We are eternal absorbers, we just absorb from everywhere. We absorb the air, knowledge, food. That's just what we do. So it's important every so often to reflect whether we are giving back, but how do we know if we're doing this?

This was a thoughtful observation, but the manager wasn't sure whether he was doing more giving than taking or that he could even tell. And how could he? We may aspire to live a good life or be good parents or community members, but how do we judge how well we are doing? There is no yardstick for answering this question.

Perhaps the answer is to rely on our best judgment. But then we run into another problem: How do we make these judgments honestly and accurately? When we look at ourselves in the proverbial mirror, we often see a nicely airbrushed image. At other times, we judge ourselves harshly and become victims of what psychoanalysts call the *punitive superego*. As one therapist put it, "Were we to meet this figure socially, this accusatory character, this internal critic, this unrelenting fault finder, we would think there was something wrong with him. He would be just boring and cruel."[2]

Seeing ourselves as we are is the most challenging aspect of measuring up. An avalanche of experience and evidence—from serious literature, the long historical record, the wisdom of many different faiths, and the findings of contemporary social science—tell us that we routinely do a poor job of seeing ourselves as we are. If we had a scale for measuring up, our thumb would be on it most of the time.

So how do we reflect on measuring up and do it well? A useful answer says to follow some combination of three approaches. Each is a way of reflecting, briefly or at length. Each has deep roots in the long history of serious thought about reflection. Taken together, the three approaches can help you reflect on how well your actions are matching up with your obligations and aspirations.

## Rely on Companions and Guides

The first step in closing this gap is to put aside the standard advice to rely on your true self or your moral compass. In *Hamlet*, Shakespeare provided the most famous version of this approach when he wrote, "To thine own self be true."[3] But Shakespeare put these words into the mouth of Polonius, a garrulous busybody and something of a fool, suggesting we should think twice about this advice.

When we do this, we find that the "true self" approach is riddled with problems. Sometimes, when we face a hard decision, we don't know what our "true self" is telling us to do. That is precisely what makes some decisions hard. In other words, how do we follow our "moral compass" when it is swinging back and forth? If we look back honestly, we also see that our strong convictions have sometimes led us in the wrong direction.[4]

Oscar Wilde, the Irish playwright, said somewhat flippantly, "Only the shallow know themselves." But poets and novelists, as well as theologians and philosophers, repeatedly remind us about the complexities, treacheries, and subtleties of our selves.[5] As one philosopher put it, "Both self and consciousness invite a sense of mystery."[6]

When they talked about measuring up, the men and women I interviewed rarely referred to finding or relying on their true selves. Instead, several of them relied explicitly on companions and guides. These were actual individuals they had known personally or knew a great deal about—and who provided lived, practical, on-the-ground standards for measuring up.

For example, one manager, who had been a US state governor and a federal cabinet official, said he believed in treating everyone equally. And then, without prompting, he said he learned what this meant from his father and described a particular incident from his boyhood:

My father was waiting on an African American customer one day, and one of his big clients, a contractor, came in and said, "I need such and such." My father said, "OK, as soon as I help Mr. So-and-so, I'll get to you." The guy waited two or three minutes, and he said, "I said I needed this." My father said, "Well, I'm helping him." The contractor said, "You're going to help this [n-word] before you help me?" My father answered, "No. No, I'm going to help him, and I'm not going to help you. You need to go take your business somewhere else."

What should we make of this story? Standing alone, it looks like a simple, inspirational anecdote. However, if we put it in the context of the long history, it is a clear example of a valuable way to handle the challenge of measuring up without a yardstick. You can see this by looking at what Marcus Aurelius wrote in the very first pages of his *Meditations*.

Here you find a passage that is easy to overlook because it resembles the standard acknowledgments at the start of many books. In this passage, Marcus thanks thirteen individuals. Some are people whose counterparts we can imagine, like his father, mother, and brother. Others, like Diognetus and Alexander the Platonic, seem utterly obscure. But Marcus knew all of them, and his first book thanks each of them for specific traits, inclinations, and examples that they provided for him.

He begins by thanking his grandfather for teaching him "the government of my temper" and his mother for showing him "simplicity in my way of living, far removed from the habits of the rich." Marcus continues by thanking others for providing examples of values, attitudes, and behavior he admired and wanted to emulate. He concludes by remembering his father, and writing, "In my father I observed mildness of temper, and unchangeable resolution in the things which he had determined after due deliberation; and no vainglory in those things which men call honours; and a love of labour and perseverance; and a readiness to listen to those who had anything to propose for the common weal."[7]

We may, like Marcus, aspire to be courageous, honest, and responsible. But Marcus took an important further step. He focused sharply on particular individuals and specific aspects of their behavior, and he had observed them personally. They gave him clear, flesh-and-blood examples of what would otherwise be lofty, inspiring, but nearly contentless values and ideals.

Marcus was hardly alone in following this approach to measuring up. Ignatius was deeply familiar with the lives of Catholic saints. Montaigne drew on his own unique, secular pantheon of philosophers, poets, and statesmen, most of whom lived in ancient Greece or Rome. General George Patton had a personal mental assembly of great generals. He understood their lives, the wars they fought, and their tactics and strategies in particular battles. He tried hard to emulate them and felt crushed when he felt he had failed.[8] Important political and social movements typically have exemplars and heroes whose decisions, commitments, and actions exemplify the defining values of their causes.

Companions and guides are valuable because we can ask ourselves what they would have done in situations we are facing. Where would they have set the bar? Can we find ways to act that parallel or embody what we saw them do in similar situations? One manager followed this approach explicitly. He said, "I had a bunch of mentors, good and bad, and I ask myself how would this one or that one think about something, what would they do, and why would they do it?"

Companions and guides provide customized standards and personalized incentives to meet the standards. Some scholars believe that Marcus's assembly of admirable individuals served him as a jury.[9] He could look through their eyes and compare his actions to theirs. He may have also felt accountable for meeting the standards they exemplified because he knew these individuals and respected them.

For Marcus, measuring up was not just a day-by-day or action-by-action approach. He was also concerned about the cumulative development of his character. Put differently, he wanted to become a certain kind of person, and his personal catalog of everyday exemplars helped him do this. They were benign enablers of his personal development. As one scholar put it, "Marcus is presenting not a usual genealogical tree of aristocrats (as we might easily expect from a Roman emperor), but a very individual and private catalogue of people around him, who mark the genealogy, the development, and the formation of his own mind, intellect, and soul."[10]

This basic approach has been validated again and again throughout the long history. Scholars of religion have written, for example, that many of the major faiths have some version of the Christian saints. These are men and women who have achieved a high degree of holiness or blessedness. Generalizations that cross cultures are hazardous, so one scholar has emphasized what he calls "family resemblances" shared by the versions of saint-hood in different religions, and his first two are serving as role models and as teachers.[11]

Many of the managers, like the former governor who recounted his father's reaction to the racist customer, took similar approaches. When they referred to the values and standards they aspired to live by, they often moved from overarching, aspirational, but indeterminate language to recollections of particular individuals and incidents. Several of the managers had a unique twist on this approach. They had worked with individuals they viewed as negative role models and consciously try to avoid their traits and behavior. One manager said, "That's not the kind of person I want to become, and I don't want to behave that way."

Companions and guides can take many different forms, but they all have an important common element. They don't rely on broad principles, noble sentiments, or heroic figures on pedestals. The managers who relied on this way of measuring up didn't look far above themselves for guidance and inspiration. They looked instead to their left and right—to learn from people they knew well and could observe closely.

## Craft Your Own Precepts

Developing your own precepts for making decisions and acting on them is a second basic way of measuring up without a yardstick. What does this mean in practice? In one of the interviews, a police chief gave this example:

My father was from the Depression—born in 1913—and he was a sergeant in the army, and he was in for a long time, and then he was a supervisor on the subway system. I remember talking to him about it, and I don't know how we ever got on the subject of supervising or managing people, and he just said to me, "You know, people don't have to like you. But people have to know that you're a fair person."

And that's really all he said, and I've always kept that with me. I always understand that we're human beings, and we can't expect ourselves to be perfect twenty-four hours a day, and we mess up. And a lot depends on how you deal with that mess-up. I remember him saying over and over again that, "Not everyone's gonna be your friend, but just be fair."

The police chief relied on his father as a companion and guide, but he took another step and relied on his father's simple precept. In fact, he said, "I don't know how many times that's gone in and out of my mind in my entire life, but it has to be a million times. And he was hardly alone in doing this. In their interviews, several managers referred to their own personal maxims for measuring up:

> You will make mistakes, but the character-based ones are the ones you can't recover from.

> I don't think you can wait until you feel right. I think you have to ask, "What do I want to do or change?" and then start practicing, and I think that over time your feelings will change.

> After you've done your praying, get out in the world and start doing things.

> I ask myself if I'm coming clean with myself.

> I travel a lot and end up juggling a thousand things, and then I remember what my father always told me, "The only thing that is certain in this life is that you're going to die."

Crafting your own basic precepts isn't a literary exercise. To do this well, you have to think deeply and focus sharply on what really matters to you. One manager called these practical, guiding precepts "promises to himself." You have to whittle away everything that is peripheral and marginal. You are trying to state the essence of the essence, in a pithy form that has an unambiguous, practical meaning for you.

Montaigne did this so well that many of his guiding precepts are widely quoted. For example:

A man who fears suffering is already suffering from what he fears.

Lend yourself to others, but give yourself to yourself.

On the highest throne in the world, we still sit only on our own bottom.[12]

Marcus took the same approach. Two of his biographers wrote, "This was a man of action, not merely of words, and the few words he wrote to himself are meant to incite actions, not dissertations . . . They contain the landmarks and lighthouses by which he navigated a life."[13] Here are some of Marcus's basic life principles:

Concentrate on what you have to do. Fix your eyes on it. Remind yourself that your task is to be a good human being; remind yourself what nature demands of people. Then do it, without hesitation, and speak the truth as you see it. But with kindness. With humility. Without hypocrisy.[14]

Ignatius took the tactic of creating personal precepts even further. He distilled one of his guiding principles into the single Latin word *magis*. In its standard use, the word simply means "more." But for Ignatius, it meant a personal standard of trying to do more, day by day and hour by hour, to give glory to God.

The classics and the interviews suggest several ways to craft personal precepts. One is to see whether some of your companions and guides suggest precepts that mean something to you. You can look for two different types of personal precept: some state how you want to live and behave, while other specify lines you don't want to cross. Try to distill your precepts into the simplest possible terms, like the police chief's mantra "Be fair, be fair." And try to stay away from precepts that are easy to follow. By setting a low bar, they can help you feel good about yourself, but they ignore Marcus's observation that "The true principles of action sting."[15]

Finally, you can follow Marcus's example and rephrase your precepts from time to time, to keep them fresh and relevant to your life. One scholar said Marcus searched "for that version which, at a given moment, would produce the greatest effect, in the moment before it fades away. The goal is to re-actualize, rekindle, and ceaselessly reawaken an inner state which is in constant danger of being dominated or extinguished . . . dispersed in the futility of routine."[16]

A few of the managers went even further and relied on highly pragmatic tactics to remind themselves of their aspirations, their role models, and their guiding precepts. They wanted to raise the odds that these signals penetrated the persistent ambient noise of life today. This was their version of a tactic Montaigne used: he had his favorite precepts for living well painted on the exposed beams of the chamber where he wrote *Essays*.

For example, one of the managers was a practicing Buddhist and had signed up for an email program that sent him a Buddhist adage for the day. Some, he said, were centuries old, some were humorous, and none was straightforward, so he had to pause and reflect to understand them. One, for example, said, "Don't shift the ox's burden to the cow," which he interpreted as saying not to shift what you are responsible for on to others. He said, "You look at the message, and you say, 'Oh, OK. How am I doing with that?'" He also acknowledged that this could sound gimmicky, but he felt that the alternative for him was going home at the end of the day and thinking, "I didn't reflect at all today."

One woman relied on a creative, personalized version of a standard to-do list. Every morning, she wrote down what she had to do and wanted to do that day, and she included a short period of reflection and sometimes a question or saying that she wanted to spend time reflecting on. She was actually creating a "to-live" list, and not a "to-do" list, because it nudged her to think briefly about her standards, her values, and her life while she was handling her tasks for the day.

## Step Back Further

Measuring up is reflection with a focus on action—on doing, rather than experiencing or understanding. It relies on tactics, like everyday role models and personal precepts, to help you meet your standards and aspirations in the here and now. From time to time, however, it is important to step back further. This can give you a deeper perspective on how you are measuring up.

Here is how one manager described this perspective:

I think you need, and this is especially true for leaders who have far more things vying for their attention than they could ever possibly focus on, what I call "an architecture for your life."

The architecture asks: What are those things that I am going to do every single day that are really important to me, as a person, as a husband, father, whatever? What are the things that I'm going to do every day? What are the things that I'm going to do every week, every month, that kind of define the structure of my life?

This way of stepping back further and measuring up is simple yet profound. It tells us to view our daily activities as building blocks in a larger structure. The American writer Annie Dillard explained the importance of this perspective matters when she wrote, "How we spend our days is, of course, how we spend our lives."[17]

We have seen important examples of this approach in the classical literature on reflection. Montaigne organized the architecture of his days around a quest to record, with full honesty, his thoughts and feelings. Ignatius constructed a life of holiness and religious fidelity. Marcus worked daily to sculpt his worldview, character, and daily behavior in accord with the stoic model.

What does stepping back further mean in practice? The basic answer is simple. It means stepping back for more than just a few moments or minutes. It also means broadening the horizons of your reflection—that is, shifting them from the nearer term to the longer run—and then trying to grasp what really matters.

Roughly half of the managers did find time for longer periods of reflection, although many of them wished they could do this more often than they did. Several other managers were practicing members of religious faiths, and they emphasized the importance of regular religious services. A Hindu manager spent ten days every January at a meditation retreat, and during the rest of the year, he tried to meditate and reflect for an hour each morning. The managers who weren't religious also understood the importance of stepping back further, and they did this in a wide variety of ways. Some went for walks on weekends, spent time listening to music, or just sat quietly with a cup of coffee or tea or a glass of wine. One manager, for example, tried to follow a simple formula. He aimed "to reflect ten minutes a day, one hour a week, and one day a year."

For other managers, stepping back further wasn't a solitary exercise. When they really needed to grapple with significant question about their lives, they turned to someone they knew and trusted for long, broad-ranging, reflective conversations about their concerns.

In a few cases, managers said they did what was, in effect, a hybrid combination of extended and mosaic reflection. For example, one executive said he sometimes had to make what he knew was an important decision but didn't yet know what to do. When this happened, he made sure to close his office door and think quietly about the decision, sometimes for as long as thirty minutes. If this didn't resolve the uncertainty, then he basically "carried the decision around" for a while. He would come back to it from time to time, for brief periods. Sometimes this gave him a new perspective; sometimes he realized he was going in circles. In the end, of course, he had to make a decision, but he grappled with these hard problems by combining extended, solitary deliberation with a mosaic approach.

How did the managers know when to step back further? They relied on several different triggers. One was facing a high-stakes decision at work or elsewhere in their lives. Another was going through an important life event, like losing a job or suffering from a serious illness. Sometimes they felt life was spinning out of control and they needed to hit the brakes. Sometimes a question or concern had been lurking in the back of their minds, so they put aside time to confront it directly. As the psychologist Maurice Riseling observed, "Sooner or later, life makes philosophers of us all."[18]

You can step back further to see if you are really measuring up, and you can also do it as a way of downshifting or pondering in greater depth. For example, the aim of reflection as downshifting or contemplation is depth of experience. The brief, mosaic version of this kind of reflection means grasping what really matters about something you are experiencing now. It is being present and attentive to whatever is happening around you or inside you. But stepping back further can help you do this in a deeper or even more profound way.

You can see this by contrasting popular, contemporary forms of meditation with their original versions in Asian religions and cultures. Our standard view of meditation is *mindfulness*. This is spending ten or fifteen minutes emptying your mind and paying attention to your breath. Studies show that this can lower blood pressure, calm nerves, and improve concentration. But mindfulness meditation has little in common with ancient practices. These required longer periods of time, and their aim wasn't health, calm, or productivity. It was glimpsing or experiencing some profound reality inside ourselves or in the world around us—realities usually obscured by our rational minds, our need to get things done, and our continuous efforts to understand, navigate, and control the world around us.

During the last century, the German diplomat and psychologist Karlfried Dürckheim was an early proponent of the Japanese tradition of Zen Buddhism. In his book, *The Japanese Cult of Tranquility*, he explains this tradition in terms of a "deeper self" within us and a "greater life" surrounding us. For Dürckheim and many other interpreters of Eastern meditative traditions, these profound realities cannot be grasped by brief "time-outs" from pressing everyday activities. He also stresses that Western religious traditions have a similar orientation, telling the faithful that true life is what these traditions sometimes call "the repose of the soul in God," and teaching that this requires extended periods of prayer and devotion.[19]

Each of the approaches to downshifting can be extended in ways that can deepen a person's inner life. For example, one approach was trying to spend a few moments glimpsing nature, perhaps by doing something as simple as looking out a window or spending a moment or two looking at a screen saver of an outdoor scene. These are examples of tiny mosaic tiles, but it is also possible to look at nature or the sky for longer periods—in other words, to step back further—and deepen the experience. For example, the astronomer Carl Sagan described the Earth as seen from a distant satellite. Our planet appeared as a tiny, "pale blue dot," and yet, Sagan wrote, "Everyone you love, everyone you know, everyone you ever heard of, every human being who ever was, lived out their lives . . . on a mote of dust suspended in a sunbeam."[20]

Like contemplation, pondering sometimes requires longer periods of time. The hard situations, in life and at work, are blurry and gray. These are the problems that managers take home with them at night, not in their briefcases or laptops, but in the backs of their minds. And everyone faces these problems—as parents, partners, citizens, employees, or simply as human beings trying to understand a problem or situation. These problems gnaw at us, distract us during the day, and sometimes keep us awake at night—usually because there are many different and sometimes conflicting ways of seeing these problems. You have to turn them over in your mind slowly, patiently, and repeatedly—sometimes over an extended period or several periods of time—to understand their full complexity.

Pondering can also be a way of examining the great, enduring questions of life. If we extend our horizons beyond the specks of embodied consciousness we call ourselves, we confront questions that some of the managers, when they were speaking with particular candor, said mattered most to them: Why are we here? Is there a God? What gives life meaning? For centuries, philosophers and theologians have pondered these questions, as have men and women in every walk of life.

Finding longer periods for reflection requires a degree of discipline. It is no surprise that Marcus, a wartime military commander, or Ignatius, who spent his early years as a soldier, held this belief. But even Montaigne, who often tried to soften the demands of his conscience, believed firmly in will and discipline. "Not being able to govern events," he wrote, "I govern myself."[21]

Fortunately, we human creatures seem to have an instinct for stepping back, so we don't have to rely solely on willpower. This instinct probably originated with our ancient ancestors: early humans who could learn from the past and plan for the future were more likely to survive, and they eventually evolved into us. Other evidence for this innate inclination includes the many cultures and traditions around the world that have their own ways of practicing the art of reflection. And the interviews point in the same direction. Virtually all of the managers had developed personal ways of stepping back, despite their very busy lives, just as Marcus, Montaigne, and Ignatius did.

Yet several basic themes run through all this variety. Reflection is stepping back to grasp what really matters about what we are experiencing, trying to understand, or doing. You can reflect in three fundamental ways—by downshifting, pondering, and measuring up. Spending time this way will enhance your life and your work—if you develop a pattern or mosaic of reflection that meshes with your life and if you occasionally step back further and reflect more deeply.

Without reflection, we drift. Others shape and direct us. With reflection, we can understand and even bend the trajectories of our lives.

# Appendix

# Research Process

This short book emerged from a long and extensive research effort that focused on two basic questions. We often hear that we should spend more time reflecting, and we sometimes give versions of this advice to others. But what is reflection? And how can busy men and women find time to do it?

The research proceeded on two tracks. One was extensive background reading on reflection and related topics. The bibliography indicates the broad scope of this work—because the topic of reflection is multidimensional and can be understood from many important and thought-provoking perspectives. In the end, my notes on this reading became a sprawling literature review, roughly nine hundred single-spaced pages long. It was eventually organized into roughly twenty topics, each covering a broad area such as classic views of reflections, obstacles to reflection, philosophical perspectives, and neuroscience.

This background reading confronted a serious challenge. Reflection is very difficult to study because it is an elusive phenomenon. You can't put it under a microscope and observe it directly. In addition, reflection is conceptually linked to deeply vexed issues like human consciousness: we have scant knowledge of how consciousness evolved, what it is, or how it arises from the matter in our brains.

Hence, my basic approach to understanding reflection was triangulation. The extensive literature review was one part of this effort. I also read a number of important diaries, as well as books on the whole phenomenon of diaries and journals, since these are, in essence, frozen reflection. Finally, to improve the accuracy of the triangulation, I moved beyond reading and pursued a second research track.

This consisted of more than one hundred interviews with managers. Most of them were participants in various Harvard Business School executive education programs. They had volunteered to be interviewed in response to personal emails from me, and I sent the invitations to participants who would represent a wide range of backgrounds.

In addition, I interviewed roughly twenty-five other individuals. Some were senior Harvard Business School staff members. For the most part, these were individuals I had known for years and had sometimes worked with, and I chose them because I was curious to see if an established personal relationship would be conducive to more open conversations. I also interviewed faculty colleagues who had spent most of their careers working in and often leading companies and other organizations, as well as several well-known CEOs and former CEOs who visited the school's campus as speakers. Finally, to broaden the range of perspectives on reflection, I interviewed several therapists, religious counselors, a long-time practitioner and teacher of Buddhism, a university president, a police chief, and a well-known European football coach.

In the end, a third of the interviewees were women. A quarter were non-Americans. Two-thirds were between the ages of forty and sixty, a few were older, and the rest were earlier in their careers. Two-thirds were senior middle managers, and the rest, with the exception of five early-career managers, were former CEOs or heads of their organizations.

## Appendix

The interviews fell into two phases. The first involved the initial fifty interviews. I interviewed each of these individuals twice, about two weeks apart. The first interview raised a series of topics—described below—and the second interview returned to these topics, to see if the interviewees had any further thoughts. Also, between their two interviews, I emailed each participant and asked them to describe any type of reflection they had done during the last day or so. My aim was getting a "real-time," everyday sample of reflection.

During the second phase of interviews, I met with each individual just once. I shifted to this approach because I was able to focus the interviews more effectively, given what I had learned in the first phase and because I now had a sharper focus for the research. In both phases, the interviews typically lasted an hour or more, they took place in my office, and the conversations were recorded with the permission of the interviewees and later transcribed. The interviews and transcriptions were and are confidential. Ultimately, I accumulated more than two thousand pages of transcription.

The interviews were open-ended and conversational. In some cases, I shared some of my own preliminary thinking about reflection and some of what I have learned from previous interviews. In each interview, I tried to cover certain questions, but I also departed from my prepared questions to pursue interesting or potentially important side paths.

My prepared questions for the first interview were: What, as you see it, is reflection? What comes to mind when you think about reflection? In what ways is reflection valuable and in what ways can it be a problem? When and how do you typically reflect? What questions or issues do you typically focus on? What are you trying to accomplish when you reflect? What are the main obstacles to reflection for you? Do you feel you spend enough time reflecting?

The email questions for the first fifty interviewees were: In the last few hours, did you spend any time reflecting? What did you reflect on? When and how did you do it? In the second round of questions with these interviewees, I planned to ask: Is there anything you would like to add to what we covered in our first conversation? How do you assess how well you are reflecting? Do you think you reflect differently on professional issues, as opposed to personal ones? How do you tell the difference between useful reflection and brooding—and is brooding sometimes worthwhile? If you had more time for reflection, how would you spend it? What role, if any, does religion or spirituality play in your reflection?

## Appendix

Writing the final manuscript was surprisingly time-consuming. In hindsight, I see that the basic problem was finding a way to distill what was important in the thousands of pages of background notes and interview transcripts. I wanted to write a book that was short, useful, and easily accessible. As a result, I had to work my way through two challenging tasks. One was discerning the central themes running through the notes and transcripts. These themes ultimately became the four design principles for reflection.

The other ongoing challenge was excising from initial drafts of the manuscript a large number of insightful comments from the interviewees and important perspectives on reflection from the background notes—simply because other perspectives seemed even more valuable. In the end, I probably wrote at least five times as many words, in a series of preliminary drafts, as now appear in the final version of the book.

Despite my best efforts, the book almost certainly contains errors of fact and interpretation, and they are my responsibility.

# NOTES

## Chapter 1

1. Pierre Hadot, *The Inner Citadel: The* Meditations *of Marcus Aurelius* (Cambridge, MA: Harvard University Press, 2001), 313.

2. The twentieth-century painter and design theorist Maitland E. Graves was a modern pioneer in the effort to articulate fundamental principles of visual and spatial aesthetics. His landmark work is *The Art of Color and Design* (Columbus, OH: McGraw-Hill, 1941).

3. Interaction Design Foundation, "Design Principles," https://www.interaction-design.org/literature/topics/design -principles.

## Chapter 2

1. The phrase "good enough," as it is now used in a variety of contexts with the meaning presented here, was first utilized in this fashion by the psychoanalyst D. W. Winnicott. See D. W. Winnicott, Lesley Caldwell, and Helen Taylor Robinson (eds.), *The Collected Works of D. W. Winnicott*, vol. 6 (Oxford: Oxford University Press, 2016), 321–324. Winnicott's aim was to protect families raising children from the excessive impact of professional expertise and ideal notions of good motherhood. The phrase was later popularized by the child psychologist Bruno Bettleheim in *A Good Enough Parent* (New York: Alfred A. Knopf, 1987).

2. Many writers across many centuries have expressed variations on this theme. Voltaire's version—"The perfect is the enemy of the good"—is probably the most famous, and all can be viewed as interpretations of Aristotle's "golden mean."

3. Captain Renault to Rick, *Casablanca*, Julius and Philip Epstein, screenwriters, Hollywood, CA: Hal B. Wallis Production, 1942.

4. Henry David Thoreau, *Walden and "Civil Disobedience"* (New York: Signet Classics, 2002), 74.

5. Arthur Schopenhauer, *Counsels and Maxims* (New York: Cosimo Classics, 2007), 25.

6. Anna Katharina Schaffner, *Exhaustion: A History* (New York: Columbia University Press, 2017).

7. Tony Schwartz and Christine Porath, "Why You Hate Work," *New York Times*, May 30, 2014.

8. An overview of these findings is Anandi Mani et al., "Poverty Impedes Cognitive Function," *Science* 341, no. 6149 (August 2013): 976–980.

9. Silvia Bellezza, Neeru Paharia, and Anat Keinan, "Conspicuous Consumption of Time: When Busyness and Lack of Leisure Time Become a Status Symbol," *Journal of Consumer Research* (June 2017).

10. Daniel Halévy, *My Friend Degas* (Middletown CT: Wesleyan University Press, 1964), 119.

11. Andy Jones-Wilkins, "Running as Reflection," *Irunfar*, September 20, 2013, http://www.irunfar.com/2013/09/running-as-reflection.html.

12. A brief account of Marcus's responsibilities, his physical limitations, and his devotion to his work is Marcus Aurelius, *The Emperor's Handbook: A New Translation of* The Meditations, trans. David Hicks and C. Scot Hicks (New York: Scribner, 2002), 6–10. Marcus wrote *The Meditations* under such dire circumstances that his thoughts often turned to death. See Anthony Birley, *Marcus Aurelius* (London: Eyre & Spottiswoode, 1966), 293–299.

13. Marcus Aurelius, *Meditations*, trans. A. S. L. Farquharson (New York: Alfred A. Knopf, 1992), 48.

# Notes

## Chapter 3

1. The ancient Greeks also prized contemplation, and some scholars believe that the standard version of Aristotle's definition of human beings—defining them as "rational animals"—is mistaken and that a better translation would be "contemplative animals." For example, Hannah Arendt wrote, "Aristotle meant neither to define man in general nor to indicate man's highest capacity, which to him was not logos, that is, not speech or reason, but nous, the capacity of contemplation, whose chief characteristics is that its content cannot be rendered in speech." See Hannah Arendt, *The Human Condition* (Chicago: University of Chicago Press, 1998), 27.

2. Henry David Thoreau, *Walden and "Civil Disobedience"* (New York: New American Library, 1960), 66.

3. Philippe Desan, *The Oxford Handbook of Montaigne* (Oxford: Oxford University Press, 2016), 763.

4. A comprehensive account of the wide variety of meditation techniques and the current, limited state of understanding of the neurophysical processes underlying meditation is Antoine Lutz, John D. Dunne, and Richard J. Davidson, "Meditation and the Neuroscience of Consciousness," in *Cambridge Handbook of Consciousness*, ed. P. Zelazo, M. Moscovitch and E. Thompson (Cambridge: Cambridge University Press, 2017). A similar treatment is John S. Strong, *Buddhisms: An Introduction* (London: Oneworld, 2015).

5. John Lubbock, *The Use of Life* (New York: The Macmillan Company, 1900), 69.

6. There is a vast literature, scientific as well as popular, on the default mode network and its implications. A serious, technical, but accessible introduction is Mary Helen Immordino-Yang, Joanna A. Christodoulou, and Vanessa Singh, "Rest Is Not Idleness: Implications of the Brain's Default Mode for Human Development and Education," *Perspectives on Psychological Science* 7, no. 4 (2012): 352–364.

7. Marilynne Robinson, *Gilead* (New York: Picador, 2006), 179.

# Notes

8. Frank Jakubowsky, *Whitman Revisited* (Bloomington, IN: WestBow Press Publishing, 2012), 10.

9. See Jonathan Miller, *On Reflection* (London: National Gallery of Art, 1998). Phenomenology, an important school of modern philosophy, has examined and displayed the stunning complexity of "the present moment" and our consciousness of it. For an overview, see Shaun Gallagher and Dan Zahavi, "Phenomenological Approaches to Self-Consciousness," *The Stanford Encyclopedia of Philosophy* (Winter 2016 Edition), ed. Edward N. Zalta, https://plato.stanford.edu/archives/win2016/entries/self-consciousness-phenomenological/.

10. Terrence Cave, *How to Read Montaigne* (London: Granta Books, 2013), 67.

11. An overview of the extensive research on rumination is in Susan Nolen-Hoeksema, Blair Wisco, and Sonja Lyubomirsky, "Rethinking Rumination," *Perspectives on Psychological Science* 3, no. 5 (2008): 400–424, doi:10.1111/j.1745-6924.2008.00088.x. PMID 26158958.

12. David Johnson, *A Quaker Prayer Life* (San Francisco: Inner Light Books, 2013), 16.

13. David Lilienthal, *The Harvest Years: 1959–1963* (New York: Harper & Row, 1964), 124.

14. Anaïs Nin, *Mirages: The Unexpurgated Diary of Anaïs Nin, 1939–1944* (Athens, OH: Swallow Press, 2013), 22.

15. Anne Frank, *The Diary of a Young Girl*, trans. Susan Massotty (New York: Everyman's Library, 2010).

16. Proust is reported to have said this in conversation. See Alain de Botton, *How Proust Can Change Your Life* (New York: Vintage, 1998), 45.

17. Donald Frame, *Montaigne: A Biography* (New York: Harcourt, Brace & World, 1965), 283.

18. See Edward O. Wilson, *Biophilia* (Cambridge, MA: Harvard University Press, 1984), and Stephen R. Kellert and Edward O. Wilson, *The Biophilia Hypothesis* (Washington, DC: Shearwater, 1995).

19. Centers for Disease Control and Prevention, "Healthy Pets and Healthy People," https://www.cdc.gov/healthypets/index.html. Studies today provide varying perspectives on windows and recovery time in hospitals. See, for example, Wen-Chun Chiu et al., "The Impact of Windows on the Outcomes of Medical Intensive Care Unit Patients," *International Journal of Gerontology* 12, no. 1 (March 2018): 67–70, and Cleveland Clinic, "A Room with a View: Do Hospital Window Views Affect Clinical Outcomes?," *Consult QD*, https://consultqd.clevelandclinic.org/room-view-hospital-window-views-affect-clinical-outcomes/.

20. Joseph N. Tylenda, *A Pilgrim's Journey: The Autobiography of Ignatius of Loyola* (San Francisco: Ignatius Press, 2001), 130.

21. Gerard Manley Hopkins, "God's Grandeur," *God's Grandeur and Other Poems* (New York: Dover Publications, 1995), 15.

22. One scholar of ancient Roman and Greek philosophy argues at length that contemplation was central to Marcus's way of thinking and living. See Pierre Hadot, *What Is Ancient Philosophy?* (Cambridge, MA: Harvard University Press, 2002), especially p. 176ff.

23. Marcus Aurelius Antoninus, *The Meditations of the Emperor Marcus Aurelius Antoninus*, trans. Francis Hutcheson (Carmel, IN; Liberty Fund, 2007), 66.

24. James Boswell, *Life of Johnson* (Oxford: Oxford University Press, 1998), 957.

25. Michel de Montaigne, *Montaigne: Selected Essays*, trans. James B. Atkinson and David Sices (Indianapolis: Hackett Publishing, 2012), 272.

26. For an overview, see Amrisha Vaish, Tobias Grossmann, and Amanda Woodward, "Not All Emotions Are Created Equal: The Negativity Bias in Social-Emotional Development," *Psychological Bulletin* 134, no 3 (May 2008): 383–403.

27. Adam Phillips, *Unforbidden Pleasures* (New York: Farrar, Straus, and Giroux, 2015), 85.

28. Aura, "A Simple Productivity Weapon by Andreessen: The Anti-to-Do List," *Business Insider*, June 14, 2016,

# Notes

https://medium.com/business-startup-development-and-more/a
-simple-productivity-weapon-by-andreessen-the-anti-to-do-list
-1fee961c3b72.

29. Versions of the White Rabbit's statement have been attributed to many different people, but its original version seems to be the Disney film. See https://quoteinvestigator.com/2014/03/22 /stand-there/.

30. Michel de Montaigne, *Montaigne's Selected Essays and Writings*, ed. and trans. Donald M. Frame (New York: St Martin's Press, 1963), 447.

31. Pico Iyer, *The Art of Stillness* (New York: Simon & Schuster, 2014), 61.

## Chapter 4

1. John Keats, *The Complete Poetical Works and Letters of John Keats*, ed. Horace Elisha Scudder (Boston and New York: Houghton Mifflin, 1899), 277.

2. Daniel Kahneman, *Thinking, Fast and Slow* (New York: Farrar, Straus and Giroux, 2011).

3. For further details on Montaigne's often challenging activities during his "retirement," see Richard Scholar, *Montaigne and the Art of Free-Thinking* (Oxford: Peter Lang, 2010), 1–3; Donald Frame, *Montaigne: A Biography* (New York: Harcourt, Brace & World, 1965), 130–131; and Ullrich Langer, "Montaigne's Political and Religious Context," *The Cambridge Companion to Montaigne* (Cambridge: Cambridge University Press, 2005).

4. Michel de Montaigne, *The Works of Montaigne*, ed. William Hazlitt (London: C. Templeman, 1845), 206.

5. Scholar, *Montaigne and the Art of Free-Thinking*, 98.

6. Hugo Friedrich, *Montaigne* (Berkeley: University of California Press, 1991), 122.

7. Donald Frame, *Selections from the Essays of Montaigne* (New York: Appleton-Century-Crofts, 1948), 18.

8. See Martin E. P. Seligman et al., *Homo Prospectus* (Oxford: Oxford University Press, 2016).

# Notes

9. See Marcus Aurelius Antoninus, *The Meditations of the Emperor Marcus Aurelius Antoninus*, vol. 1, trans. and ed. A. S. L. Farquharson (Oxford: Clarendon Press, 1944), 309. Others make the broader claim that all diaries are addressed to an interlocutor, if only unconsciously. See Thomas Mallon, *A Book of One's Own: People and Their Diaries* (New York: Ticknor and Fields, 1984).

10. See J. Michael Sparough, Tim Hipskind, and Jim Manney, *What's Your Decision? How to Make Choices with Confidence and Clarity* (Chicago: Loyola Press, 2010), 39–41.

11. Thomas Merton, *The Inner Experience: Notes on Contemplation* (New York: HarperOne, 2003), 2.

12. Timothy D. Wilson, *Strangers to Ourselves: Discovering the Adaptive Unconscious* (Cambridge, MA: Belknap Press, 2002).

13. Blaise Pascal, *Pensées and Other Writings*, trans. Honor Levi (Oxford: Oxford University Press, 1995), 158.

14. Dennis Overbye, "Brace Yourself! Here Comes Einstein's Year," *New York Times*, January 25, 2005, https://www.nytimes.com/2005/01/25/science/brace-yourself-here-comes-einsteins-year.html.

15. Menachem Z. Rosensaft, ed., *God, Faith, and Identity from the Ashes: Reflections of Children and Grandchildren of Holocaust Survivors* (Nashville, TN: Jewish Lights Publishing, 2014).

16. Ibid., 203.

17. Ratnaguna, *Art of Reflection* (Cambridge: Windhorse Publications, 2018), 68.

18. The commonly quoted version of what Proust wrote—"The real voyage of discovery consists not in seeking new lands but seeing with new eyes"—is actually a significant rewriting and compression of Proust's actual words. One English translation of the original French is:

> A pair of wings, a different respiratory system, which enabled us to travel through space, would in no way help us, for if we visited Mars or Venus while keeping the same senses, they would clothe everything we could see in the same aspect as the things of the Earth. The only true voyage, the only bath in the Fountain of Youth, would be not

to visit strange lands but to possess other eyes, to see the universe through the eyes of another, of a hundred others, to see the hundred universes that each of them sees, that each of them is; and this we do, with great artists; with artists like these we do really fly from star to star.

See Marcel Proust, *In Search of Lost Time*, vol. 5, trans. C. K. Scott Moncrief and Terence Kilmartin (New York: Modern Library, 1993), 343.

## Chapter 5

1. Thomas Carlyle, *Sartor Resartus* (Oxford: Oxford University Press, 1999), 201.

2. Adam Phillips, "Against Self-Criticism," *London Review of Books*, March 5, 2015, 14.

3. William Shakespeare, *The Tragical History of Hamlet, Prince of Denmark* (London: Adam & Charles Black, 1911), act 1, scene 3, 78–82.

4. For an overview of the philosophical and personal challenges associated with the idea of the "true self," see Stephen Hetherington, *Self-Knowledge* (Peterborough, Ontario: Broadview Press, 2007); and Qaassim Cassam, *Self-Knowledge for Humans* (Oxford: Oxford University Press, 2015).

5. Oscar Wilde, *The Writings of Oscar Wilde* (London: A. R. Keller & Co., 1907), 142.

6. Robert C. Solomon, *Spirituality for the Skeptic: The Thoughtful Love of Life* (Oxford: Oxford University Press, 2002), 10.

7. Marcus Aurelius, *Meditations*, trans. Gregory Hayes (New York: Modern Library, 2002), 102.

8. Martin Blumenson, *The Patton Papers* (Boston: Da Capo Press, 1996), chapter 11.

9. See Irmgard Männlein-Robert, "The *Meditations* as a (Philosophical) Autobiography," in *A Companion to Marcus Aurelius*, ed. Marcel van Ackeren (Hoboken, NJ: Wiley-Blackwell, 2012), 369–370.

10. Männlein-Robert, "The *Meditations* as a (Philosophical) Autobiography." See also Michael Erler, "Aspects of Orality in (the Text of) the *Meditations*," in *A Companion to Marcus Aurelius*, 346–349.

11. John A. Coleman, "Conclusion: After Sainthood," in *Saints and Virtues*, ed. John Stratton Hawley (Berkeley: University of California Press, 1987), 214–217.

12. These are examples of the many contemporary translations of Montaigne's pithy guidance, and these versions appear in https://www.brainyquote.com/authors/michel_de_montaigne.

13. Marcus Aurelius, *The Emperor's Handbook: A New Translation of* The Meditations, trans. David Hicks and C. Scot Hicks (New York: Scribner, 2002), 4. See also Angelo Giavatto, "The Style of *The Meditations*," in *A Companion to Marcus Aurelius*, ed. Marcel van Ackeren (Hoboken, NJ: Wiley-Blackwell, 2012): 333–345.

14. Marcus Aurelius, *Meditations*, trans. Hayes, 1–6.

15. Marcus Aurelius, *The Essential Marcus Aurelius*, trans. Jacob Needleman and John P. Piazza (London: Penguin Group, 2008), 10:34.

16. Pierre Hadot, *The Inner Citadel*: The Meditations *of Marcus Aurelius* (Cambridge, MA: Harvard University Press, 2001), p. 51.

17. Annie Dillard, *The Writing Life* (New York: Harper-Perennial, 1989), 32.

18. Maurice Riseling, quoted in Solomon, *Spirituality for the Skeptic,* 26.

19. Karlfried Dürckheim, *The Japanese Cult of Tranquility* (York Beach, ME: Samuel Weiser, 1991), 1–18.

20. Carl Sagan, *Pale Blue Dot* (New York: Ballentine Books, 1994), 6.

21. Michel de Montaigne, *The Works of Michael de Montaigne*, ed. William Hazlitt (Philadelphia: J. W. Moore, 1849), 327.

# BIBLIOGRAPHY

Arendt, Hannah. *The Human Condition*. Chicago: University of Chicago Press, 1998.

Aura. "A Simple Productivity Weapon by Andreessen: The Anti-to-Do List." *Business Insider*, June 14, 2016. https://medium.com /business-startup-development-and-more/a-simple-productivity -weapon-by-andreessen-the-anti-to-do-list-1fee961c3b72.

Bakewell, Sarah. *How to Live: Or a Life of Montaigne in One Question and Twenty Attempts at an Answer*. London: Chatto and Windus, 2011.

Barth, J. Robert. "Mortal Beauty: Ignatius Loyola, Samuel Taylor Coleridge, and the Role of Imagination in Religious Experience." *On Christianity and Literature* 50, no. 1 (Autumn 2000): 69–78.

Batchelor, Stephen, Christina Feldman, Akincano M. Weber, and John Peacock. "What Mindfulness Is Not." *Tricycle: The Buddhist Review*, September 17, 2018. https://tricycle.org/trikedaily /mindfulness-buddhism/.

Bellezza, Silvia, Neeru Paharia, and Anat Keinan. "Conspicuous Consumption of Time: When Busyness and Lack of Leisure Time Become a Status Symbol." *Journal of Consumer Research* (June 2017).

Bettleheim, Bruno. *A Good Enough Parent*. New York: Alfred A. Knopf, 1987.

Birley, Anthony. *Marcus Aurelius*. London: Eyre & Spottiswoode, 1966.

# Bibliography

Blumenson, Martin. *The Patton Papers*. Boston: Da Capo Press, 1996.

Boswell, James. *Life of Johnson*. Oxford: Oxford University Press, 1998.

de Botton, Alain. *How Proust Can Change Your Life*. New York: Vintage, 1998.

Bowler, Kate. "How Cancer Changes Hope." *New York Times*, December 28, 2018. https://www.nytimes.com/2018/12/28/opinion/sunday/resolutions-hope-cancer-god.html.

Buckner, Randy L., Jessica R. Andrews-Hanna, and Daniel L. Schechter. "The Brain's Default Network: Anatomy, Function, and Relevance to Disease." *Annals of the New York Academy of Science* 1124 (2008): 1–38.

Burke, Peter. *Montaigne*. Oxford: Oxford University Press, 1981.

Carlyle, Thomas. *Sartor Resartus*. Oxford: Oxford University Press, 1999.

Cassam, Quassim. *Self-Knowledge for Humans*. Oxford: Oxford University Press, 2015.

Cave, Terrence. *How to Read Montaigne*. London: Granta Books, 2013.

Centers for Disease Control and Prevention. "Healthy Pets and Healthy People." https://www.cdc.gov/healthypets/index.html.

Chiu, Wen-Chun, Po-Shuo Chang, Cheng-Fang Hsieh, Chien-Ming Chao, and Chih-Cheng Lai. "The Impact of Windows on the Outcomes of Medical Intensive Care Unit Patients." *International Journal of Gerontology* 12 (March 2018): 67–70.

Cleveland Clinic. "A Room with a View: Do Hospital Window Views Affect Clinical Outcomes?" *Consult QD*. https://consultqd.clevelandclinic.org/room-view-hospital-window-views-affect-clinical-outcomes/.

Csikszentmihalyi, Mihaly. *Flow: The Psychology of Optimal Experience*. New York: HarperCollins Publishers, 1991.

Curtiz, Michael, dir. *Casablanca*. Hollywood, CA: Hal B. Wallis Production, 1942.

Desan, Philippe. *The Oxford Handbook of Montaigne*. Oxford: Oxford University Press, 2016, 763.

Dewey, John. *How We Think.* Lexington, MA: D.C. Heath, 1933.

Dillard, Annie. *The Writing Life.* New York: Harper Perennial, 1989.

Dürckheim, Karlfried. *The Japanese Cult of Tranquility.* York Beach, ME: Samuel Weiser, 1991.

Farquharson, A. S. L. *The Meditations of the Emperor Marcus Aurelius Antoninus*, vol. 1. Oxford: Clarendon Press, 1944.

Flanigan, Owen. *The Bodhisattva's Brain.* Cambridge, MA: MIT Press, 2011.

Fleming, David L. *What Is Ignatian Spirituality?* Chicago: Loyola Press, 2008.

Frame, Donald. *Montaigne: A Biography.* New York: Harcourt, Brace & World, 1965.

————. *Selections from the Essays of Montaigne.* New York: Appleton-Century-Crofts, 1948.

Frampton, Saul. *When I Am Playing with My Cat, How Do I Know She Is Not Playing with Me?* London: Faber and Faber, 2011.

Frank, Anne. *The Diary of a Young Girl.* Translated by Susan Massotty. New York: Everyman's Library, 2010.

Friedrich, Hugo. *Montaigne.* Berkeley, CA: University of California Press, 1991.

Gallagher, Shaun, and Dan Zahavi. "Phenomenological Approaches to Self-Consciousness." In *The Stanford Encyclopedia of Philosophy*, edited by Edward N. Zalta. Winter 2016 Edition. https://plato.stanford.edu/archives/win2016/entries/self-consciousness-phenomenological/.

Gardner, Ryan S., and Michael K. Freeman. "'Serious Reflection' for Religious Educators." *Religious Educator* 12, no. 3 (2011): 59–81.

George, Bill. *True North: Discover Your Authentic Leadership.* San Francisco: Jossey-Bass, 2007.

Giavatto, Angelo. "The Style of *The Meditations*." In *A Companion to Marcus Aurelius*, edited by Marcel van Ackeren, Hoboken, NJ: Wiley-Blackwell, 2012, 333–345.

Graves, Maitland E. *The Art of Color and Design*. Columbus, OH: McGraw-Hill, 1941.

Guevara, Ernesto Che. *The Bolivian Diaries: Authorized Version*. Minneapolis, MN: Ocean Press, 2005.

Van Gulik, Robert. "Consciousness." In *The Stanford Encyclopedia of Philosophy*, edited by Edward N. Zalta. Winter 2016 Edition. https://plato.stanford.edu/archives/spr2018/entries/consciousness/.

Hadot, Pierre. *The Inner Citadel: The* Meditations *of Marcus Aurelius*. Cambridge, MA: Harvard University Press, 2001.

——. *What Is Ancient Philosophy?* Cambridge, MA: Harvard University Press, 2002.

Halévy, Daniel. *My Friend Degas*. Middletown, CT: Wesleyan University Press, 1964.

Hammarskjöld, Dag. *Markings*. Translated by Lief Sjoberg. New York: Vintage Books, 2007.

Hart, William. *Vipassana Meditation: The Art of Living*. Maharashtra, India: Vipassana Research Institute, 2014.

Hazlitt, William, ed. *The Works of Montaigne*. London: C. Templeman, 1845.

Hetherington, Stephen. *Self-Knowledge*. Peterborough, Canada: Broadview Press, 2007.

Hickman, Martha Whitmore. *Healing After Loss: Daily Meditations for Working Through Grief*. New York: William Morrow Paperbacks, 1994.

Hopkins, Gerard Manley. "God's Grandeur." *God's Grandeur and Other Poems*. New York: Dover Publications, 1995.

"The Human Brain Is the Most Complex Structure in the Universe." *Independent*, April 2, 2014. https://www.independent.co.uk/voices/editorials/the-human-brain-is-the-most-complex-structure-in-the-universe-let-s-do-all-we-can-to-unravel-its-9233125.html.

Immordino-Yang, Mary Helen, Joanna A. Christodoulou, and Vanessa Singh. "Rest Is Not Idleness: Implications of the Brain's Default Mode for Human Development and Education." *Perspectives on Psychological Science* 7, no. 4 (2012): 352–364.

# Bibliography

Interaction Design Foundation. "Design Principles." https://www
.interaction-design.org/literature/topics/design-principles.

Iyer, Pico. *The Art of Stillness*. New York: Simon & Schuster, 2014.

Jakubowsky, Frank. *Whitman Revisited*. Bloomington, IN: West-
Bow Press Publishing, 2012.

Johnson, Alexandra. *A Brief History of Diaries: From Pepys to
Blogs*. London: Hesperus Press, 2011.

Johnson, David. *A Quaker Prayer Life*. San Francisco: Inner Light
Books, 2013.

Jones-Wilkins, Andy. "Running as Reflection." *Irunfar*, September 20, 2013. http://www.irunfar.com/2013/09/running-as
-reflection.html.

Kahneman, Daniel. *Thinking, Fast and Slow*. New York: Farrar,
Straus and Giroux, 2011.

Keats, John. *The Complete Poetical Works and Letters of John
Keats*, edited by Horace Elisha Scudder. Boston and New
York: Houghton Mifflin, 1899.

Kellert, Stephen R., and Edward O. Wilson. *The Biophilia Hypothesis*. Washington, DC: Shearwater, 1995.

Koepnick, Lutz. *On Slowness: Toward an Aesthetic of the Contemporary*. New York: Columbia University Press, 2014.

Kohn, Edward P., ed. *A Most Glorious Ride: The Diaries of Theo-
dore Roosevelt, 1887–1886*. Albany, NY: State University of New
York Press, 2015.

Kreiner, Jamie. "How to Reduce Digital Distractions: Advice
from Medieval Monks." *Aeon*, April 24, 2019. https://aeon
.co/ideas/how-to-reduce-digital-distractions-advice-from
-medieval-monks.

Kress, Jill M. "Contesting Metaphors and the Discourse of Consciousness in William James." *Journal of the History of Ideas* 61,
no. 2 (April 2000): 263–283.

Langer, Ullrich. "Montaigne's Political and Religious Context."
In *The Cambridge Companion to Montaigne*. Cambridge: Cambridge University Press, 2005.

Lilienthal, David. *The Harvest Years: 1959–1963*. New York:
Harper & Row, 1964.

Long, Christopher R., and James R. Averill. "Solitude: An Exploration of Benefits of Being Alone." *Journal for the Theory of Social Behavior* 33, no. 1 (2003): 21–44.

Lubbock, John. *The Use of Life.* New York: Macmillan, 1900.

Lutz, Antoine, John D. Dunne, and Richard J. Davidson. "Meditation and the Neuroscience of Consciousness." In *The Cambridge Handbook of Consciousness*, edited by Philip David Zelazo, Morris Moscovitch, and Evan Thompson. Cambridge: Cambridge University Press, 2017, 497–550.

Mallon, Thomas. *A Book of One's Own: People and Their Diaries.* New York: Ticknor and Fields, 1984.

Mani, Anandi, Sendil Mullainathan, Eldar Shafir, and Jiaying Zhao. "Poverty Impedes Cognitive Function." *Science* 341, no. 6149 (August 2013): 976–980.

Manney, Jim. *An Ignatian Book of Prayers.* Chicago: Loyola Press, 2014.

Männlein-Robert, Irmgard. "*The Meditations* as a (Philosophical) Autobiography." In *A Companion to Marcus Aurelius*, edited by Marcel van Ackeren. Hoboken, NJ: Wiley-Blackwell, 2012, 362–381.

Marcus Aurelius. *The Emperor's Handbook: A New Translation of the* Meditations. Translated by David Hicks and C. Scot Hicks. New York: Scribner, 2002.

———. *The Essential Marcus Aurelius.* Translated by Jacob Needleman and John P. Piazza. London: Penguin Group, 2008.

———. *Meditations.* Translated and edited by A. S. L. Farquharson. New York: Alfred A. Knopf, 1992.

———. *Meditations.* Translated by Gregory Hayes. New York: Modern Library, 2002.

Marcus Aurelius Antoninus. *The Meditations of the Emperor Marcus Aurelius Antoninus.* Translated by Francis Hutcheson. Carmel, IN: Liberty Fund, 2007.

Matsushita, Konosuke. *My Way of Life and Thinking.* Kyoto, Japan: PHP Institute, 2011.

McCarthy, Molly. *The Accidental Diarist: A History of the Daily Planner in America*. Chicago: University of Chicago Press, 2013.

Meissner, William. *Ignatius of Loyola: The Psychology of a Saint*. New Haven, CT: Yale University Press, 1994.

Menary, Richard, ed. *The Extended Mind*. Cambridge MA: MIT Press, 2012.

Merton, Thomas. *The Inner Experience: Notes on Contemplation*. New York: HarperOne, 2003.

Miller, Jonathan. *On Reflection*. London: National Gallery of Art, 1998.

Moberg, Dennis, and Martin Calkins. "Reflection in Business Ethics: Insights from Saint Ignatius's Spiritual Exercises." *Journal of Business Ethics* 33 (2001): 257–270.

de Montaigne, Michel. *The Complete Essays*. Translated by M. A. Screech. London: Penguin Books, 2003.

———. *Montaigne's Selected Essays and Writings*. Translated and edited by Donald M. Frame. New York: St Martin's Press, 1963.

———. *The Works of Montaigne*. Edited by William Hazlitt. London: C. Templeman, 1845.

Nagel, Thomas. "What Is It Like to Be a Bat?" *The Philosophical Review* 83, no. 4 (October 1974): 435–450.

Neustadt, Richard E., and Ernest R. May. *Thinking in Time: The Uses of History for Decision-Makers*. New York: Free Press, 1988.

Nielsen, Jared A., Brandon A. Zielinski, Michael A. Ferguson, Janet E. Lainhart, and Jeffrey S. Anderson. "An Evaluation of the Left-Brain vs. Right-Brain Hypothesis with Resting State Functional Connectivity Magnetic Resonance Imaging." *PlosOne* 8, no. 8 (August 14, 2013). https://journals.plos.org/plosone/article?id=10.1371/journal.pone.0071275.

Nin, Anaïs. *Mirages: The Unexpurgated Diary of Anaïs Nin, 1939–1944*. Athens, OH: Swallow Press, 2013.

Nolen-Hoeksema, Susan, Blair Wisco, and Sonja Lyubomirsky. "Rethinking Rumination." *Perspectives on Psychological Science*

3, no. 5 (2008): 400–424. doi:10.1111/j.1745-6924.2008.00088.x. PMID 26158958.

Neuroskeptic. "The 70,000 Thoughts Per Day Myth?" *Discover: Science for the Curious*. http://blogs.discovermagazine.com/neuroskeptic/2012/05/09/the-70000-thoughts-per-day-myth/#.

Overbye, Dennis. "Brace Yourself! Here Comes Einstein's Year." *New York Times*, January 25, 2005. https://www.nytimes.com/2005/01/25/science/brace-yourself-here-comes-einsteins-year.html.

Pang, Alex Soojung-Kim. *Rest: Why You Get More Done When You Work Less*. New York: Basic Books, 2016.

Parker-Pope, Tara. "Writing Your Way to Happiness." *New York Times*, January 19, 2015. https://well.blogs.nytimes.com/2015/01/19/writing-your-way-to-happiness/.

Pascal, Blaise. *Pensées and Other Writings*. Translated by Honor Levi. Oxford: Oxford University Press, 1995.

Phillips, Adam. "Against Self-Criticism." *London Review of Books*, March 5, 2015.

———. *Unforbidden Pleasures*. New York: Farrar, Straus and Giroux, 2015.

Popper, Karl. *Of Clouds and Clocks*. St. Louis, MO: Washington University, 1966.

Proust, Marcel. *In Search of Lost Time*, vol. 5. Translated by C. K. Scott Moncrief and Terence Kilmartin. New York: Modern Library, 1993.

Ratnaguna, *Art of Reflection*. Cambridge: Windhorse Publications, 2018.

Ravier, André. *Ignatius of Loyola and the Founding of the Society of Jesus*. San Francisco: Ignatius Press, 1987.

Reiser, William. "The Spiritual Exercises in a Religiously Pluralistic World." *Spiritus: A Journal of Christian Spirituality* 10, no. 2 (Fall 2010).

Robinson, Marilynne. *Gilead*. New York: Picador, 2006.

Rosensaft, Menachem Z., ed. *God, Faith, and Identity from the Ashes: Reflections of Children and Grandchildren of Ho-*

*locaust Survivors*. Nashville, TN: Jewish Lights Publishing, 2014.

Rutherford, R. B. *The Meditations of Marcus Aurelius: A Study*. Oxford: Clarendon Press, 1991.

Sagan, Carl. *Pale Blue Dot*. New York: Ballentine Books, 1994.

Sayce, Richard A. *The Essays of Montaigne: A Critical Exploration*. London: Weidenfeld and Nicolson, 1972.

Schaffner, Anna Katharina. *Exhaustion: A History*. New York: Columbia University Press, 2017.

Schissel, Lillian. *Women's Diaries of the Westward Journey*. New York: Schocken Books, 2004.

Schmitz, James H. "The Altruist." *Galaxy Science Fiction*, September 1952.

Scholar, Richard. *Montaigne and the Art of Free-Thinking*. Oxford: Peter Lang, 2010.

Schopenhauer, Arthur. *Counsels and Maxims*. Translated by T. Bailey Saunders. New York: Cosimo Classics, 2007.

———. *Essays of Arthur Schopenhauer*. Translated by T. Bailey Saunders. New York: A. L. Burt Company, 1902.

Schwartz, Tony and Christine Porath. "Why You Hate Work." *New York Times*, May 30, 2014. https://www.nytimes.com/2014/06/01/opinion/sunday/why-you-hate-work.html.

Seligman, Martin E. P., Peter Railton, Roy F. Baumeister, and Chandra Sripada. *Homo Prospectus*. Oxford: Oxford University Press, 2016.

Shakespeare, William. *The Tragical History of Hamlet, Prince of Denmark*. London: Adam & Charles Black, 1911.

Sharf, Robert H. "Is Mindfulness Buddhist? (and Why It Matters)." *Transcultural Psychiatry* 52, no. 4 (2015): 470–484.

Sedikides, Constantine, Rosie Meek, Mark D. Alicke, and Sarah Taylor. "Behind Bars but Above the Bar: Prisoners Consider Themselves More Prosocial Than Non-Prisoners." *British Journal of Social Psychology* 53, no. 2 (December 2013): 396–403.

Smith, David Woodruff. "Phenomenology." In *The Stanford Encyclopedia of Philosophy*, edited by Edward N. Zalta. Winter

2016 Edition. https://plato.stanford.edu/archives/sum2018
/entries/phenomenology/.

Solomon, Robert C. *Spirituality for the Skeptic: The Thoughtful Love of Life*. Oxford: Oxford University Press, 2002.

Sparough, J. Michael, Tim Hipskind, and Jim Manney. *What's Your Decision? How to Make Choices with Confidence and Clarity*. Chicago: Loyola Press, 2010.

Stoljar, Natalie. "Feminist Perspectives on Autonomy." In *The Stanford Encyclopedia of Philosophy*, edited by Edward N. Zalta. Winter 2016 Edition. https://plato.stanford.edu/archives /win2018/entries/feminism-autonomy/.

Strong, John S. *Buddhisms: An Introduction*. London: Oneworld, 2015.

Taylor, Alan, and Irene Taylor, eds. *The Assassin's Cloak: An Anthology of the World's Greatest Diarists*. Edinburgh: Canongate Books, 2011.

Taylor, Charles. *The Ethics of Authenticity*. Cambridge, MA: Harvard University Press, 2018.

Thich Thien-an. *Zen Philosophy, Zen Action*. Cazadero, CA: Dharma Publishing, 1975.

Thoreau, Henry David. *Walden and "Civil Disobedience."* New York: New American Library, 1960.

Traub, George W. "Six Characteristics of Ignatian Spirituality." *Ignatian Spirituality.com*. http://www.ignatianspirituality.com /what-is-ignatian-spirituality/six-characteristics-of-ignatian -spirituality.

Treanor, Brian, and Brendan Sweetman. "Gabriel (-Honoré) Marcel." In *The Stanford Encyclopedia of Philosophy*, edited by Edward N. Zalta. Winter 2016 Edition. https://plato .stanford.edu/archives/win2016/entries/marcel/.

Tylenda, Joseph N. *A Pilgrim's Journey: The Autobiography of Ignatius of Loyola*. San Francisco: Ignatius Press, 2001.

Vaish, Amrisha, Tobias Grossmann, and Amanda Woodward. "Not All Emotions Are Created Equal: The Negativity Bias in Social-Emotional Development." *Psychology Bulletin* 134, no. 3 (May 2008): 383–403.

Wallace, B. Alan. *Mind in the Balance: Meditation in Science, Buddhism, and Christianity.* New York: Columbia University Press, 2007.

"What Is Ignatian Spirituality?" Ignatian Spirituality.com. http://www.ignatianspirituality.com/what-is-ignatian-spirituality/.

"What Mindfulness Is Not." *Tricycle: The Buddhist Review*, September 17, 2018. https://tricycle.org/trikedaily/mindfulness-buddhism/.

Wikipedia. "Christian Contemplation," last edited on January 15, 2020. https://en.wikipedia.org/wiki/Christian_contemplation.

Wilde, Oscar. *The Writings of Oscar Wilde.* London: A. R. Keller & Co., 1907.

Wilson, Edward O. *Biophilia.* Cambridge, MA: Harvard University Press, 1984.

Wilson, Timothy D. *Redirect: Changing the Stories We Live By.* New York: Little, Brown and Company, 2011.

———. *Strangers to Ourselves: Discovering the Adaptive Unconscious.* Cambridge, MA: Belknap Press, 2002.

Winnicott, D. W., Lesley Caldwell, and Helen Taylor Robinson, eds. *The Collected Works of D. W. Winnicott*, vol. 6. Oxford: Oxford University Press, 2016.

Wright, Robert. *Why Buddhism Is True: The Science and Philosophy of Meditation and Enlightenment.* New York: Simon and Schuster, 2018.

# INDEX

# Index

# Index

# Index

# Index

# ACKNOWLEDGMENTS

I am grateful to many friends and colleagues who took time from very busy schedules to read parts or all of the draft of this book and made innumerable valuable suggestions for improving it—particularly Sam Lam, Nitin Nohria, Julianne Nolan, and Ken Winston. My daughters, Maria, Luisa, and Gabriella, read versions of the manuscript, some riddled with problems, and helped with corrections and suggestions. My wife, Patricia O'Brien, provided many helpful ideas as well as crucial guidance for framing the book. Finally, my editor, Kevin Evers, and my literary agent, Raphael Sagalyn, also provided practical and insightful guidance at every step in the process.

I am also grateful to the men and women who participated in the interviews on which this book it based. Their thoughtful, honest accounts of when and how they reflected taught me a great deal and, in the end, made this book possible.

## Acknowledgments

Finally, I want to thank the generous alumni of Harvard Business School who provided the resources that made this work possible.

# ABOUT THE AUTHOR

**JOSEPH L. BADARACCO** is the John Shad Professor of Business Ethics at Harvard Business School. He has taught courses on business ethics, strategy, and management in the school's MBA and executive programs. Badaracco is a graduate of St. Louis University; Oxford University, where he was a Rhodes scholar; and Harvard Business School, where he earned an MBA and a DBA. He has written nine other books on leadership, responsibility, and decision making, and these books have been translated into twelve languages.